World Book Myths & Legends Series

SOUTH AMERICAN MYTHS & LEGENDS

AS TOLD BY PHILIP ARDAGH

ILLUSTRATED BY SYRAH ARNOLD

World Book, Inc.
a Scott Fetzer company
Chicago

MYTH OR LEGEND?

Long before people could read or write, stories were passed on by word of mouth. Every time they were told, they changed a little, with a new character added here and a twist to the plot there. From these ever-changing tales, myths and legends were born.

WHAT IS A MYTH?

In early times, people developed stories to explain local customs and natural phenomena, including how the world and humanity developed. These myths were considered sacred and true. Most include superhuman beings with special powers.

WHAT IS A LEGEND?

A legend is very much like a myth. The difference is that a legend is often based on an event that really happened or a person who really existed in relatively recent times.

THE SOUTH AMERICAN CONTINENT

South America is the fourth biggest continent in the world. It makes up about 12 percent of the earth's land. For a continent so vast, its population is quite small, with only about 6 percent of the world's people. The biggest country in South America is Brazil. Other countries include Chile, Peru and Colombia. Today most South Americans live in big cities, but the myths and legends in this book come from the peoples of the continent's mountains, forests, and grasslands.

CONTRASTING CLIMATES

Forty percent of South America is tropical, with high temperatures and a humid climate. Parts of Peru and Chile, however, are among the driest places on the planet.

DIFFERENT PEOPLES, DIFFERENT MYTHS

The European conquest of South America began in the 16th century. Because of this European influence, most modern South Americans live in towns and cities and are Christians. Before the conquest the Inca people were probably the most powerful South Americans. Many other small groups were scattered across the continent–each with its own myths and legends.

HOW DO WE KNOW?

There are still some South Americans, especially the peoples of the rain forest, who practice their old beliefs. It is important to remember that what are seen by some people as myths and legends are seen by others as their religion. Many of these myths and legends were recorded by the conquering Europeans.

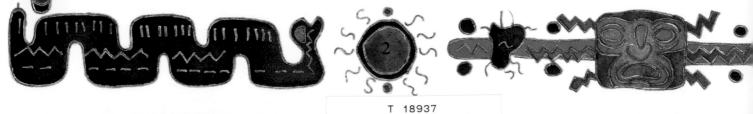

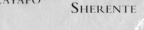

The myths and legends in this book were told by different South American peoples. This map shows where these peoples lived. The Inca Empire, whose boundaries are shown with a red line, grew up over time. Here it is shown at the height of its power (1438–1525).

KAYAPÓ

SHERENTE

CARAJÁ

BORORO

TUPINAMBA

INCA EMPIRE

This map also shows the variety of landscapes found in South America. Much more of the continent used to be rain forest —a source of food and shelter for both people and animals.

Mountains
Deserts
Rain forest
Grasslands

NOTE FROM THE AUTHOR

Myths and legends from different cultures were told in different ways. The purpose of this book is to tell new versions of these old stories, not to try to copy the way in which they were first told. I hope that you enjoy them and that this book will make you want to find out more about the South Americans and their myths and legends.

THE MYTHS & LEGENDS OF SOUTH AMERICA

The different native peoples of South America—sometimes called South American Indians—have a huge number of different myths and legends, told in hundreds of different languages. Many of these stories have common themes.

SHARED BELIEFS

Ancient South American civilizations had a similar approach to the way they saw the world around them. Mountains, rivers, plants, and animals were all seen as having supernatural and magical significance. Although there were some differences between peoples, myths and legends often had common themes.

SHARED MYTHS

One myth, shared by many groups, is that all food grew from one tree. When the tree was cut down, all the different fruits fell from its branches, and all the waters of the world sprang from its trunk.

THE INCA EMPIRE

The Inca were a people who built an empire along the Andes Mountains down the west coast of South America. Their empire stretched from present-day Ecuador, and included parts of present-day Peru, Bolivia, Chile, and Argentina.

THE CONQUERING INCA

The Inca took many of the myths and legends of the South American groups they conquered and shaped them to fit their own beliefs.

THE POWER OF POTTERY

Early peoples, dating back to 800 B.C., used pottery, textiles, gold, and silver to express their mythic beliefs. They produced paintings, patterns, and carvings to show events and characters from their myths and legends.

MIXED MYTHS

Animals also play an important role in South American myths and legends. Myths about trickster turtles are an example of how myths from different parts of the world have become intertwined. Some experts think these myths were based on tales brought to South America by African American slaves, who were forced to work for white Europeans in South America and the Caribbean.

THE IMPORTANCE OF GOLD

Gold was seen as sacred by many South American peoples, including the Inca, because they linked the gleaming brightness of gold to the brilliant rays of the sun. The conquering Spaniards had a different reason for wanting gold–greed. They plundered as much Inca and South American gold as they could.

EL DORADO

El Dorado–the golden man–is an example of how belief in a legend can lead to death and destruction. The Spanish conquerors heard a legend about a South American ruler who was covered in gold each morning and washed it off in a lake at night. This lake was said to be thick with gold. The legend also claimed that offerings to the gods of golden trinkets were thrown in the lake.

European expeditions went in search of the legendary riches of El Dorado. They all failed. Many people died along the way, including many South Americans who were killed by the invaders. Sir Walter Raleigh led an English expedition which failed to find the treasure. This failure was one of the reasons why King James I had him beheaded.

This ancient South American mask of finely beaten gold represents the sun and its rays. The Inca, and those before them, worshiped sun gods.

HOW THE STARS CAME

There are many South American myths about how the stars came to fill the skies. This myth, told by the Bororo people, begins with an ordinary morning in a village.

The men of the village were hunting, so the women collected their baskets and went to gather corn to make pancakes. But they found very few cobs of corn.

"This is a very poor crop," said one woman. "I've been searching all morning, and my basket is almost empty. We must find more cobs, or our men will go hungry."

"Let's ask the little one," suggested an old woman. "He's good at finding corncobs. . . . I don't know how he does it. He's so small, and the corn is so tall, but still he manages to find cobs!"

So one of the women went back to the village to find the little boy. She found him with his grandmother, who was trying to teach her pet macaw new words. Macaws are clever birds and can learn to say all kinds of things.

"Can the little one come with us and help us to find corncobs?" the woman asked the boy's grandmother.

"Of course," replied the grandmother. "Off you go, little one."

The little one returned to the cornfield with the woman.

"See what you can find," she urged him.

Sure enough, just as the old woman had predicted, the boy found corncob after corncob after corncob until all the women's baskets were full.

The women sat down in a clearing to strip the sweet corn from the cobs. Then they found flat stones and pounded the corn to make flour.

"This will mean plenty of cakes and pancakes for our men when they return," said the old woman. "They will be pleased!"

But whenever one of the women had her back turned, the little one stole some flour for himself.

"Of course, it's not really stealing," he told himself as he hid the flour in the hollow middles of bamboo shoots. "I found most of the corncobs that this flour is made from, so most of it is rightfully mine."

Soon the little one had enough hidden away for a feast. He picked up the bamboo shoots and returned to his grandmother, who had stayed behind in the village to keep an eye on the children.

"Grandma! Grandma!" he said. "I want to have a feast with all my friends . . . and here's the flour to make the cakes. Will you cook them for me?"

He tipped the flour out of the bamboo shoots into one big pile.

His grandmother's eyes widened in surprise. "Where did you get all that corn flour from, little one?" she asked in amazement.

"Little one," cackled the macaw, mimicking her words.

"You know that I went out to collect corncobs with the women," said the boy. "I helped them find so many cobs that they have more than enough corn for the men."

"So you stole this?" demanded his grandmother.

"Oh, no," lied the boy. "They said I could take as much as I could carry."

"Carry," squawked the bird.

His grandmother frowned, and then her face broke into a smile.

"I believe you," she said and began baking cakes.

Soon the grandmother's house was full of the delicious smells of freshly cooked cakes . . . and full of children, because the little one had invited all his friends to share the feast.

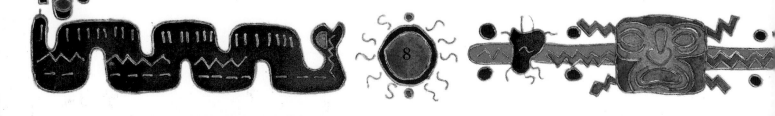

While the children ate, the boy's grandmother and her pet macaw sat in the corner and watched them fill themselves with food. She was beginning to doubt that the little one had been telling the truth. She was beginning to think that perhaps her grandson hadn't really been given the corn flour, but had stolen it.

"Is my little one a thief?" she muttered.

Her pet macaw heard the word *thief* and repeated it. "Thief!" it said, and taking a liking to the word, said it again, "Thief!"

The children fell silent.

"I don't want that silly old bird to give us away," said the little one.

"Thief!" screeched the macaw.

Without stopping to think what he was doing, the boy snatched up the bird and cut out its tongue. Some say that he then cut out his grandma's tongue to make sure that she kept quiet. But his grandma was probably frightened and upset enough not to say anything after what had happened to her poor bird.

The bad deed was done. There was no turning back. And, as so often happens, one bad thing led to another. . . . Their bellies fuller than they had been in a long time, the children swarmed out of the house after the little one and set free all the other pet macaws in the village.

Then, as slowly and as surely as the sun rises in the morning, it dawned on the little one what terrible things he had done. He had stolen the corn flour. He had cut the tongue from the bird. He had frightened his grandma. . . . Whatever next? They must flee—the children must escape before their parents found out what they'd done!

But where could they escape to where the grown-ups wouldn't find them?

"I know," said the little one. "Grown-ups aren't very good climbers because they're too heavy. Let's climb up somewhere they'll never be able to follow."

"Where?" asked a girl, with cake crumbs still around her mouth.

"To the sky!" cried the little one.

"But how?" asked an older boy.

"There are always ways!" said the little one, and just at that moment he spied a large creeper. It had big knots in its stem and would be easy for them to climb. Hovering by the creeper was a hummingbird.

The little one whispered something in the hummingbird's ear, and the tiny bird took one end of the creeper and flew with it up into the sky and fastened it in place.

"Hurry!" called out the little one and began to shin up the creeper. Soon a whole stream of children were climbing up into the heavens.

When the women returned to the village, their baskets filled with corn flour and ready to cook for their men, they found that their children were missing. They hurried to the house of the little one's grandmother. She was sobbing by her poor macaw.

"What's happened?" cried one woman.

"Where are all the children?" wailed another.

Then one of them caught sight of the legs of the very last child climbing up the creeper into the skies.

"Look! There they are!" she cried and raced off toward the creeper.

The other women followed, and soon they were all frantically climbing the knotted creeper to try to reach their children.

But the little one was right. This was a place where grown-ups would never be able to follow. The creeper could not take their weight and broke away from where the hummingbird had fastened it.

With a terrible "CRACK," the creeper dropped to earth like a coil of rope, and the women—the children's mothers, aunts, and cousins—fell screaming to the ground. But the earth was kind to them that day. Instead of all of the women being killed—and they surely would have been, because they fell from a great height—they were turned into different animals as they hit the dry, hard soil. This strange mixture of creatures then scampered, scurried, slithered, leapt, and ambled away.

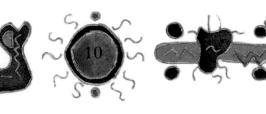

When the men returned from the hunt that night, they expected to be greeted with the smells of cooking and the cries of children, but apart from the little one's grandmother, there was no one in sight.

"Where is everyone?" one of the hunters asked the old woman.

Tongue or no tongue, the little one's grandmother was now struck completely dumb by what she had seen. She said nothing.

A few strange animals strayed aimlessly between the houses, but the men ignored them, looking around frantically for their wives, daughters, and sons.

"What could have happened to them?" asked one of the hunters. "There is no sign of attack. . . . Magic must have been at work here."

"And what are those?" cried another in surprise, pointing up into the night sky. The men of the village gasped in amazement as they looked up at the strange lights twinkling in the blackness–the lights that we now know as stars.

With the creeper gone, the children were trapped in the heavens forever. They are still there, and they never grow old. The stars are their eyes, twinkling with tears as they weep for the terrible things they did.

FIRE AND THE JAGUAR

There are many different versions of this myth among the different groups of Kayapó people, but each one tells how people learned the secret of fire and began to cook their food.

Back in the days when people dried raw meat in the sun to make it easier to chew, a man and a boy went hunting for food. The man spotted a macaw's nest high up on a rocky ledge.

"You must climb up to the nest and see if there are any eggs in it, Botoque," he told the boy.

"Why me?" asked Botoque. "You're bigger and stronger."

"Exactly," said the man. "This is a job for someone small."

Botoque tried to climb the rock face. But there weren't any handholds or footholds. "This is hopeless!" he groaned.

"Don't be so quick to give up!" said the man, who was Botoque's sister's husband. "We must make you a ladder."

The man searched around the scrub until he spotted a fallen tree trunk. "Here," he said. "Help me drag this into the opening."

With a pair of macaws circling in the sky above them, squawking out their warning cries, Botoque and his brother-in-law began cutting footholds into the dead wood to make a ladder.

When it was finished, the man and boy dragged the tree trunk up to the rock face and leaned the ladder against it.

Botoque's eyes followed the length of the tree-trunk ladder from the very bottom right up to its tip, which only just reached the ledge where the macaws were nesting. It was a long way up.

"Do you really expect me to climb that?" he asked nervously.

"Of course," said his brother-in-law. "I will hold the bottom to keep it steady."

More than a little reluctantly, Botoque climbed up and up and up until he reached the ledge. He stepped off the ladder and looked into the nest.

"How many eggs are there?" the man called up.

Botoque couldn't believe his eyes. The nest was completely empty except for two round stones.

"None!" he shouted, leaning forward to pick up the stones.

"Then what have you got in your hands?" demanded his brother-in-law, shielding his eyes against the sun to see what Botoque was doing.

"Stones!" Botoque called down. "They must have fallen off the rock face."

"You're lying!" the man shouted. "My wife's brother is a little liar! They're two lovely macaw eggs, and you want them for yourself!"

Just as Botoque put his foot back onto the tree-trunk ladder, his brother-in-law began to shake it with rage.

"Stop that!" the boy cried out in panic. "I'm not lying." He grabbed the tree trunk with both hands, and the pair of stones fell from his grasp . . . all the way down to his furious brother-in-law.

"How dare you throw stones at me!" screamed the man as one of the stones clipped him on the side of the head. He staggered backward and let go of the ladder, which fell to the ground with a mighty "CRASH." The ladder broke in two. Perhaps Botoque's brother-in-law let go on purpose. He was certainly very angry.

Fortunately for Botoque he'd had time to scramble back onto the ledge before the ladder toppled away beneath him. But unfortunately he was now trapped high up on the ledge with no way down.

"Help!" he called out. "Help me!" But his brother-in-law ignored him and walked away.

When the brother-in-law returned to the village, he told lies about Botoque, saying that he hadn't done as he was told and had run off into the undergrowth.

Botoque was alone on the narrow cliff ledge for days. The macaws were frightened by his presence and had abandoned their nest. Cold and hungry, Botoque quickly lost weight and soon was nothing more than skin and bones, his body casting a strangely shaped shadow on the dusty ground below.

Then one day a passing jaguar—a big wild cat—caught sight of the shadow and, thinking that it was some strange creature, tried to pounce on it. Every time the jaguar pounced, Botoque pulled himself back on the ledge, so his shadow disappeared from the ground.

Puzzled, the jaguar looked up and caught sight of Botoque.

"What are you?" he asked.

"I'm a human," said Botoque.

"I didn't think humans lived in nests on rocky ledges," said the jaguar, who, like all big cats, was very steady on his paws. He made his way up the rock face where no human would have found footholds.

Botoque told the jaguar about his brother-in-law's betrayal. But when the jaguar suggested he climb on his back, Botoque was nervous.

"Trust me," said the jaguar. "It is your own kind who has betrayed you, not I. Come home with me, and you can be my son."

So Botoque climbed onto the jaguar's back, and soon they reached his home. In the middle of the floor was a jatoba log, burning brightly.

"What is that?" gasped Botoque, for he had never seen anything quite so magical. The brightly colored flames seemed to dance in front of his eyes. They crackled and gave off heat, too.

"It is called fire," said the jaguar. "We cook with it."

"Cook?" asked Botoque. He had never heard this word. Humans didn't know the secret of fire, so they ate everything raw.

"You'll soon see," said the jaguar, and he called for his wife.

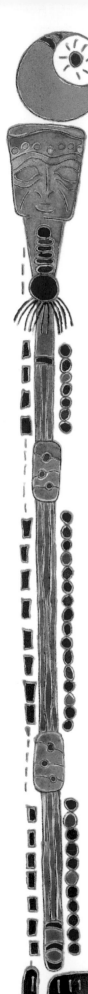

"Who is this?" asked the jaguar's wife.

"This is Botoque," said the jaguar. "He was betrayed by his own kind, so I have adopted him as our child."

"But we will soon be having a child of our own," said the jaguar's wife, who was expecting a cub. She looked at the boy by the light of the flickering flames.

"So we will have two children," said the jaguar, and that was the end of the discussion. "Now, let's eat."

And that was how Botoque became the first of his people—perhaps the first human—to eat meat cooked on a fire. It was delicious! Not only was it much easier to chew than raw meat, but the cooking brought out much more flavor. It was the best meal the boy had ever tasted. He went to sleep that night full and contented, warm in the glow of the fire.

The next morning Botoque awoke to find that the jaguar had made him a bow and arrow—a weapon no human had seen before—and the boy and animal went out hunting together. The two became very fond of each other. But the jaguar's wife was a different matter.

Whenever she and Botoque were alone together, she bared her teeth and claws. She would not let him near the meat, and sometimes he went hungry. She didn't like this new "son" in her home.

One morning, when the jaguar had gone hunting, she snarled at Botoque with such ferocity that he snatched up his bow and arrow and shot an arrow into her paw. Horrified at what he had done, Botoque felt that it was time to return to his village and to his own kind.

He grabbed a piece of cooked meat and hurried off homeward.

Back in his village there was much rejoicing from his family . . . except for his brother-in-law. Everyone had assumed Botoque was dead, yet here he was with a wondrous tale about a jaguar and something called fire. The elders tried the cooked meat and admitted that it was better than anything they'd ever tasted.

They marveled at the bow and arrow and agreed that this jaguar was, indeed, a clever fellow.

"And we must have some of this fire for ourselves," announced one of the elders. Gathering some animals around them to ask for their help, the villagers made their plans.

They crept through the forest to the jaguar's house. There a tapir heaved the burning log onto its back, and slunk back to the village with the others under the cover of darkness.

The jaguar, who had been watching them from the shadows, had a heavy heart. He had shown Botoque nothing but kindness, yet he had been betrayed. The jaguar swore never to hunt with a bow and arrow again, but to use his teeth and claws. He swore never to cook meat again, but to eat all flesh raw. The only fire he ever felt after that was a flaming rage inside him against humans–creatures who betrayed other animals as well as their own kind.

Botoque and the villagers, on the other hand, had fire to light the darkness. They could cook meat and keep warm on cold nights.

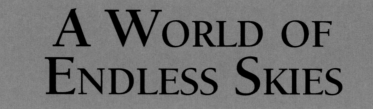

A World of Endless Skies

According to most South American myths, the first humans were immortal. They could live forever. But this Carajá myth tells a rather different story.

Long, long ago humans did not live on the surface of the earth. They lived inside it. When it was night on earth, it was daytime down below, and the reason for this was simple. When the sun set at the end of each day, it disappeared into the earth and lit this underground kingdom. Then, when it was morning, the sun rose up out of the earth and back into the sky.

Among all the people who lived in this underworld—and remember, at the beginning *all* people lived there—was one called Kaboi. Kaboi was very wise.

Sometimes he would lie on his bed at night—night down in the underworld, that is, which meant that it was daytime up on the surface—and listen to a strange cry coming from above.

Even though thick rock divided the two worlds, Kaboi could hear the cry quite clearly and wondered where it was coming from. He had no way of knowing that this was the cry of the seriema, a bird that lived on the vast grasslands of the savanna.

He had no way of knowing that the grasses themselves sang when the winds blew through them. In fact, he knew nothing of winds either, for the air in the underworld was still, and no human had ever been to the world above.

One night Kaboi could stand it no longer. He decided that he would follow the sound and try to find out where it was coming from. Several people agreed to go with him, but their names have long since been forgotten.

Kaboi and his followers climbed the rock walls of the underworld until they reached a spot where the sound was loudest.

A slight breeze blew against Kaboi's face. He had never felt a breeze before. And a new smell filled his nostrils–the smell of the grass of the savanna. Kaboi looked up, and there above him was a hole in the rock. It was a long tunnel leading to the surface.

Just then the seriema gave another cry, and the people around Kaboi cheered.

"You were right," cried one.

"You've found a way to another place!" said another with glee.

This was a very exciting moment for Kaboi. If there really was a whole new world up there, he would always be known as the one who had found the way to it.

Kaboi felt that he should say a few words to mark this important occasion, but he was too excited and hauled himself up into the entrance of the tunnel. He couldn't squeeze through the hole, though –it was very narrow, and Kaboi had a very large stomach.

"We must make the tunnel wider!" cried one.

"That won't be necessary," said Kaboi. "The most important thing is to find out what is up there," he said, pointing. "The rest of you must climb through the tunnel and explore."

They could all see how disappointed Kaboi was at not being able to visit the surface himself. But his words made sense, and the others were very eager to investigate.

Just before the last man was about to climb into the tunnel, Kaboi put his hand on his shoulder. "Don't forget to find out what makes the cry that keeps me awake at night," he said.

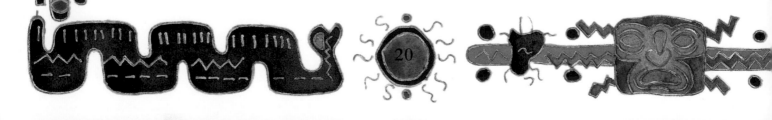

"Don't worry," said the man. "I won't."

The first people to visit the surface of the earth we now call home couldn't believe what they saw. The endless blue sky above them was like nothing they could ever have imagined. The trees, the plants, the animals, the birds. . . . Everything was so new and so exciting to their eyes.

"Kaboi has found us a paradise!" said one.

"Everyone will want to live here," said another.

"I can't wait to tell him," said another.

Someone else tried to speak, but his voice was drowned out by the cry of the seriema. "Aha!" he said in triumph when the bird had passed by. "That was the creature whose cry led us to this wondrous place. We must go back to Kaboi and report what we have found."

"We must take back things to show him, too," said the first. Everyone agreed that this was a good idea.

They gathered fruit, bees, honey, and pieces of dry wood from a dead tree; then they clambered into the tunnel to make their way back to their underground world.

"Kaboi, you have found a marvelous place," said one.

"The ceiling to the world above is not rock like the ceiling to our world, but endless blue air stretching away for as far as the eye can see," said another. He could not use the word for *sky* because no such word existed. No human had ever seen the sky–that is, until now.

Everyone started to talk at once, all eager to report the exciting things they had seen.

"Hush," said Kaboi. "There's plenty of time to discuss these things."

"Look what we brought you," said one of the search party, and they laid the fruit, bees, honey, and dry wood in front of the wise Kaboi.

Kaboi picked up a piece of fruit, smelled the skin, and bit into the flesh. Sweet juice ran down his chin. "This is delicious," he said. "It must be a wonderful world that produces such things."

Next he studied the bees and honey.

"The insects of the upper world are hard workers," he said, then bit into a piece of honeycomb, "and the results of their labor are certainly sweet. This new world is without doubt a remarkable one –a world of plenty."

Finally he picked up a piece of dry wood. He turned it over in his hands a few times. "Where was this found?" he asked.

One of the search party pushed his way to the front.

"I found it on a tree," he said.

"And are all the trees of the upper world made of wood such as this?" asked Kaboi.

"No," said the man. "The other trees grew straight and tall, with lush green leaves. This tree was lying down and had no leaves at all–which is why I brought a piece of this wood to show you."

Kaboi looked solemn. "There is no doubt that the world up there is a beautiful world. There is no doubt that it is a fruitful world. But it is also a world where everything perishes over time."

It was clear from their faces that the people did not fully understand what the wise Kaboi was saying.

"In the world above, every living thing must one day wither away and die," he explained.

"But we die here," said the man who had brought back the pieces of dry wood.

"A very different kind of death," said Kaboi. "Here we do not shrivel or dry out like this piece of dead wood. Here we are born, and we live and go on living until, after hundreds of years, we cease to be any more," said Kaboi. "Up there, things are born, they live, and they become more and more old and withered until they perish. If any of you choose to go and live in the world above, you, too, will die long before those of us wise enough to stay."

There was a puzzled silence.

Because there was no such thing as decay for our ancestors who lived in the underground world, it was very hard for them to understand what Kaboi was saying. Even many of those who did understand decided that this was a small price to pay for living in such a beautiful new world.

And so it was that many people came to tread the path up the tunnel to live on the surface of the earth, where all of us live today —with clear skies above us and the rock beneath our feet.

We are all descended from those first people who chose this new life above ground, where death comes to us all sooner rather than later.

As for Kaboi, he remained underground, content in the knowledge that he would live a longer life than those on the surface could ever imagine.

Kaboi could still hear the cry of the seriema and could picture the bird in his mind now that it had been described to him. But he heard other cries, too—of people laughing, crying, and dying.

Earth, Fire, and Flood

Throughout the world many myths and religious stories tell of great floods that represent a second chance for humankind. This Tupinambá myth is a story of earth, fire, and flood.

There was a time when the earth was completely flat without so much as a hill, valley, or mountain in sight. As far as the eye could see, there was just land. There were no seas or oceans, just enough lakes to provide all the water people needed to drink and all the water trees and plants needed to grow.

This world and its people were created and cared for by one called Monan. Monan existed before the beginning of time itself, so he had no beginning or end. He was, he is, and he will always be.

Monan treated humans like spoiled children and let them do whatever they liked, so long as they respected him as their creator and respected the earth he had created for them.

To begin with, this was a very satisfactory arrangement. Every day was a day of leisure and pleasure for his people, but as time went by, they became ungrateful.

"What do we need Monan for?" said one, as a fruit plopped into his mouth and he savored the sticky sweetness. "I wish he would leave us in peace."

"We have all we need," agreed another. "We certainly do not need Monan."

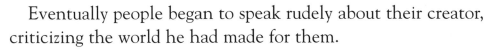

Eventually people began to speak rudely about their creator, criticizing the world he had made for them.

"I wish he'd made the days sunnier," complained one.

"I wish it weren't so bright," moaned another.

"Why is the sky such a boring blue?" said another.

Even worse, some people spoke about the earth as though it were something that had come into existence by accident. . . .They forgot about Monan altogether.

At first Monan paid no attention. He thought that his people's foolish mood would pass, and that they would soon return to being as grateful as they had been in the past. But he was wrong.

Upset at what had become of his creations, Monan turned his back on the flat earth and its inhabitants, abandoning them to life without him. But when their behavior became even more reckless, he decided that it was up to him to right the wrong.

He sent down a terrible fire from heaven. This fire, called Tara, was so hot and fierce that it not only destroyed every living thing, it also caused the earth to buckle and crease, which is how hills, valleys, and mountains came into being.

This would have been an end for all humans, had Monan not saved one person before sending down the fire. He couldn't bear the thought of destroying every one of his creations, so he saved a man called Irin-Mage.

Irin-Mage looked down on the burning earth and saw the flames reaching higher and higher.

"Do you want the flames to destroy the skies and stars, too?" he asked his creator. "If you do nothing to stop it, this fire of vengeance will soon reach us here in the heavens and destroy your own home!"

So Monan made it rain with a downpour the world had not seen the likes of before and has never seen since. Water poured from the skies like huge waterfalls, extinguishing the fires of Tara.

The fire's ashes were washed away, and the seas and oceans were formed. Mixed with the ashes, these waters became salty, which is why they are not like the fresh water of the rivers, lakes, and streams that were fed by later rains.

With its hills, valleys, mountains, oceans, and seas, the earth looked more beautiful than ever.

"I shall put you back there, Irin-Mage," said Monan. "The heavens are no place for you."

"I am grateful," said the only living human being. "You saved my life, and now you are returning me to a wonderful world . . . but I will be so lonely with no one to share it."

Monan looked kindly upon the man. "You are a good man," he said, "and I am glad that it was you that I chose to save. I will make you a wife so that she may share this new world with you. May you have many children together, for it is from you that all people will begin."

With that, Monan placed Irin-Mage and his new wife on earth.

Over time Irin-Mage and his wife had many children, but none were more powerful than their son Maira-Monan, named after the creator who had given humankind a second chance.

Maira-Monan was a great shaman, or medicine man, and knew all the secrets of nature. He liked to live on his own, but shared many of his secrets with others to help make life on earth easier. He taught the people the secret of fire and how to grow their own crops.

But Maira-Monan had even mightier powers than this. It was he who changed animals into all the different species we know today. When Monan placed Maira-Monan's parents on earth after the fire and flood, he gave them many different kinds of trees and plants, but all the animals were the same. It was Maira-Monan who used his skills to make them different. It was he who turned them into everything from armadillos and egrets to piranhas and vultures. He filled the land, water, and air with life.

Some people–and there were plenty of people by now–were frightened by Maira-Monan.

"It's all very well for him to be creating all these different kinds of animals," commented one woman. "But what if he decides to turn his attentions to us? What if he decides that we should be a different shape?"

"Or color or size?" agreed her husband.

"What if he decides we should live in the oceans like fish? Who's to stop him?" demanded the woman. "He's too powerful."

"He must be stopped!" agreed their neighbor.

"Yes!" they chanted. "Yes!"

Finally a plan was hatched, and Maira-Monan was summoned to a nearby village.

"Thank you for coming, great page," said the village leader. Page is another name for shaman. "We have something to ask of you, but first we would like you to prove your powers we have heard so much about."

"If I must," said Maira-Monan, son of Irin-Mage. Unaware that this was a trap, the idea that he had to prove his power amused him. "What do you want me to do?"

"You must walk through a number of fires that we have prepared for you," said the village leader.

"If that will satisfy you," said Maira-Monan, so they led him to the first fire.

He walked slowly through the flames–the bare soles of his feet treading on the burning embers as if they were nothing more than a few sharp pebbles–and came out the other side without so much as a smudge of ash on him.

"I don't know what that proves," said the great shaman, "but I am ready for your next fire."

So the villagers led him to the second fire. This fire contained magic that Maira-Monan was not expecting. No sooner had he stepped into the flames than he was overcome and stumbled to his knees. There were gasps from the onlookers. Had they really defeated him?

As the flames licked around Maira-Monan, he disappeared in an explosion of brilliant light followed by a noise so loud that it reached the heavens.

Those who had tricked him ran away in terror at what they had done, not knowing whether to shield their eyes or ears.

Up in the heavens the explosion reached a spirit called Tupan who caught the blinding flash and turned it into lightning and caught the rumbling "BOOM" and turned it into thunder. From that day forward Tupan became the spirit of thunder and lightning.

So every time there is a thunderstorm and lightning flashes, it is in memory of Maira-Monan. It also reminds us of the greatest storm the world has ever seen, when the creator flooded the earth and gave humans a second chance.

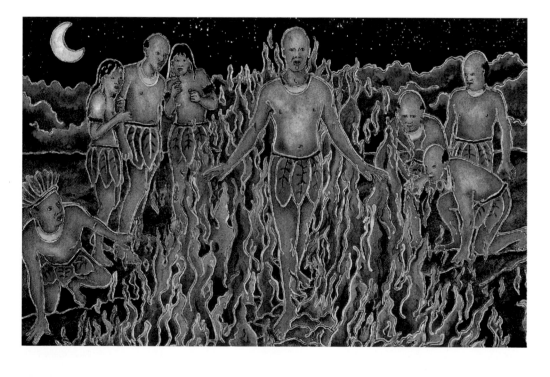

THE INCA—CHOSEN PEOPLE OF THE SUN

The fabulous Inca civilization, with its pyramid-shaped temples and wealth of gold, grew up in what is now Peru and then spread its empire up and down the Andes Mountains. This Inca myth tells where these people originally came from.

*P*acariqtambo, sometimes spelled *Paccari Tampu*, means "the place of origin" or "the dawn tavern." This was a place of three caves–three windows onto the world. Out of the middle cave stepped four brothers and four sisters, each dressed in the finest woolen shirts and blankets and each carrying beautiful vessels of the most intricately fashioned gold.

The brothers' names were Ayar Manco, Ayar Cachi, Ayar Auca, and Ayar Uchu. The four sisters were Mama Ocllo, Mama Raua, Mama Huaco, and Mama Cora. Out of the side caves came the people who were to be the ancestors of all the clans of the Inca people.

"These are the Inca, the chosen people of the Sun. They are our people," Ayar Manco told his brothers and sisters. "We must be their leaders and guide them to a land where they can live."

Ayar Manco carried a staff made of the finest gold. "We must test each place we visit with this staff," he said. "Where the staff sinks into the earth is the place where our people will settle."

The journey to find a homeland took several years, and over time the brothers and sisters grew tired of one member of their group.

Ayar Cachi was always showing off his great strength and power, and one day he went too far.

They had climbed to the top of the mountain of Huanacauri and were looking at the land spread out before them.

"Somewhere down there is a place for our people to settle and build a mighty civilization," remarked Ayar Manco.

"It is a beautiful sight," said Mama Ocllo, the eldest of the sisters.

"But not beyond improvement," said Ayar Cachi, gathering up the loose stones at his feet.

Slipping the stones into a slingshot, he began firing them at the ground below . . . with such supernatural force that they made huge dents and furrows in the landscape, creating hills and ravines where the land was once flat.

"See. Even the earth itself bends to my will!" cried Ayar Cachi.

"He is becoming too powerful for his own good," said Mama Ocllo later that day.

"He must be stopped before he turns his strength against our people," said Ayar Manco. "We must protect the children of the Sun."

"He will not simply stop if we ask him," said Mama Raua. "How can we hope to silence him?"

"We will give him an important mission," said Ayar Manco, an idea forming in his mind. "One he cannot refuse. We will ask him to return to the great opening from which we came and to bring out the sacred llama to help us on our journey."

"And?" asked Ayar Auca.

"Once he is inside, we will wall him up inside the cave where he can do no more mischief!" said Ayar Manco.

"An excellent plan," agreed Mama Cora.

So Ayar Cachi's brothers and sisters went to him. "We have an important task, and you seem the obvious one to fulfill it," said Ayar Manco, and he asked his brother to return to the cave for the llama.

"Why should I go?" demanded Ayar Cachi.

"Because you are the fastest," said a sister.

"You are the fittest," said a brother.

"You tire less quickly," said another sister.

"It is true that I am quicker, fitter, and have greater stamina than you all," said Ayar Cachi. "I can see now why you want me to be the one to return to the cave for the sacred llama. I will go."

Just as Ayar Manco had predicted, his brother's pride had made him fall into their trap.

Unaware that he was being followed, Ayar Cachi returned to the caves at Pacariqtambo. No sooner had he stepped inside the middle cave from which all eight had originally entered this world than it was sealed up behind him.

"What's happening?" he cried, banging his huge fists against the wall of rock, but the rock remained solid, and his cries echoed in his ears.

"Let me out!" he demanded. "Let me out!"

Now there were only three brothers to continue the journey with their four sisters.

Ayar Uchu made an announcement: "I have decided to stay here at Huanacauri, from where our brother Ayar Cachi threw his stones."

His sisters begged him to go with them.

"Your duty lies with us and the Inca people," said Mama Raua.

"We need you," said Mama Huaco.

"Need me, Mama Huaco?" said Ayar Uchu. "I think not. You are a far greater fighter and warrior than I could ever be. You will do fine without me. My mind is made up."

"What will you do?" asked Mama Cora.

"I will watch over our people from this high place . . . forever," he said. And as these last words passed his lips, Ayar Uchu turned to stone.

Ayar Manco put his hands to the stone. "Goodbye, brother," he said, and turned away.

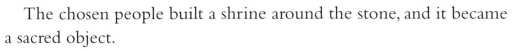

The chosen people built a shrine around the stone, and it became a sacred object.

Some say that Ayar Cachi somehow managed to escape from the cave at Pacariqtambo and that he joined Ayar Uchu on the mountaintop and that he, too, turned himself to stone. Whatever happened, only two of the four original brothers, Ayar Manco and Ayar Auca, continued their journey.

"I grow weary of traveling," Ayar Auca declared one morning. "Will we ever find a place for the Inca to settle?"

"We must and we will," said his sisters.

"But I travel better alone," said Ayar Auca.

With that he said goodbye to his brother Ayar Manco and to his sisters Mama Ocllo, Mama Raua, Mama Huaco, and Mama Cora and went his own way. Stories tell of how he eventually settled outside a city and, like his brothers before him, turned into a sacred stone.

This left Ayar Manco as the one remaining brother. It was he who went with his sisters to the valley of Cuzco. It was he who lowered the sacred golden staff to test the richness of the soil . . . and sank it right into the earth where it disappeared from view.

"Crops will grow well here," said Mama Ocllo. "This is a fertile place."

"This is the place where our people will settle and flourish," Ayar Manco announced.

"But other people already live here," Mama Cora reminded him.

"Then we must drive them away," said Mama Ocllo, who was now the mother of Ayar Manco's son, Sinchi Roca. "The Inca are the chosen people of the Sun. They need this land to grow their crops. Those already here must be made to give it up to them."

News of the arrival of the chosen people, led by Ayar Manco and his four sisters, soon spread. The people of the valley fought long and hard to defend their land, because their land was everything to them.

"They fight well," said Ayar Manco, "and they are many. How will we ever defeat them?"

"With fear," said Mama Huaco.

Ayar Uchu had been right. Mama Huaco was a great fighter and warrior. The next time the enemy attacked, she picked up her bola—stones tied together—and hurled it at her target. The bola wrapped around the man's head, killing him before he hit the ground.

The people of the valley turned and fled. Thanks to one of the four sisters from the middle cave of Pacariqtambo, the valley of Cuzco had been won for the Inca people.

After that Ayar Manco became known as Manco Capac, the founder of the Inca. It is said that he and his sisters built the first Inca homes in the valley with their own hands.

When the time came, Manco Capac turned to stone like his brothers before him. His son, Sinchi Roca, became the second emperor of the Inca—the chosen people of the Sun.

THE VOYAGE OF THE POPPYKETTLE

According to the Inca, El Niño ruled the wind, the weather, the ocean, and its creatures. El Niño was all-powerful and easily angered. This myth from Peru shows how El Niño could sometimes be kind, too.

Soon after the Spanish conquest, in a part of Peru that had been ruled by the mighty Inca before them, there lived gnomes as well as human beings . . . or so the story goes.

These gnomes wore clothes very similar to those of the Inca, who had ruled the empire, but they had long, shaggy hair and great big beards . . . great big beards for gnomes, that is. An Inca gnome's beard would barely cover the top of your thumb! And, like most gnomes the world over, these gnomes were always getting into mischief.

One day, in a place called Callo, which overlooked the sea, a small band of gnomes decided that enough was enough.

"We Inca gnomes enjoy fun," said one, "and fun is one thing we certainly don't have now that the Spaniards are our rulers. I say we should go somewhere else."

"A fine sentiment indeed," said a second gnome. "A fine sentiment. Where exactly should we go?"

"Why, there of course!" said a third, pointing to the horizon.

"What's there?" asked a fourth.

"Who knows?" said a fifth. "It would be exciting to find out."

"But how will we get there, wherever there is?" asked a sixth.

"Brown Pelican will help us," said the last member of the group of gnomes, which means—if you've been paying attention—that there must have been seven gnomes in this particular group.

Now Brown Pelican was a messenger to El Niño, lord of the weather, wind, and ocean. It was Brown Pelican's job to report to El Niño when people had been good and deserved his favor, and to report when they had been bad and deserved to be punished.

Brown Pelican liked the gnomes a lot more than he liked the Spanish invaders, but he didn't have time to fly them all the way to the horizon and beyond.

"But I will take you to Machu Picchu," said Brown Pelican.

"But why should we go there?" asked one of the gnomes.

Another one nudged him in the ribs. "Shh!" he hissed. "Or Brown Pelican might not want to take us anywhere."

"Good point," whispered a third, though he, too, wondered why the bird would want to take them to Machu Picchu—an Inca city, high in the Andes Mountains. Once this city had been full of life and color, but since the conquest it lay empty and in ruins.

"It's very kind of you to help us like this, but why Machu Picchu?" asked a fourth Inca gnome.

"You'll see," said Brown Pelican. "Climb onto my back, all of you, and hold on tight . . . but no tugging my feathers."

So the seven gnomes clambered up onto Brown Pelican's back. There was a bit of pushing and shoving as each tried to get the best view without being too near the edge. None of them wanted to fall off once they were up and away.

They landed in Machu Picchu on a ruined wall. "Here we are," said Brown Pelican. "I must be off now. Good luck with your voyage!"

"But why did you bring us here?" called out one of the bemused gnomes, still feeling rather blown about from the flight on Brown Pelican's back.

"To find you a ship," called out Brown Pelican, as he flew up into the sky. "You can't sail the seas without a ship."

"He's quite mad, you know," said one of the gnomes.

"Completely," agreed a second.

"He must be," agreed a third.

"How can we hope to find a ship up here?" asked a fourth.

"Look!" said a fifth.

"What?" asked a sixth.

"There!" said the seventh.

And they all crowded around an object resting on a nearby wall.

"It's a ship!" cried one with glee.

"Good old Brown Pelican!" cried another.

"Where are the sails?" asked a third.

"Good point!" said a fourth.

"We can make our own sails," said a fifth.

"Are you sure it's a ship?" asked a sixth.

"It's a gnome ship," said the seventh, "and a human poppykettle."

He was quite right. Made of clay, a poppykettle looks like a cross between an old-fashioned kettle and a teapot. It was used for brewing poppyseed tea. All you needed were poppyseeds, three brass keys–for flavor–and boiling water. But the seven Inca gnomes weren't about to brew up some tea. No. They set about turning the poppykettle into a ship!

When they were ready, El Niño sent them the great Silverado Bird on the wind. The gnomes had only just climbed aboard their ship–which they'd named the *Poppykettle*–when the bird swooped down, took the handle in its beak, and flew them down to the beach.

There more help was at hand, and a magical silver fish towed them out into the Pacific Ocean. Now their journey began in earnest.

A fair wind blew them toward the horizon, thanks to a little help from El Niño.

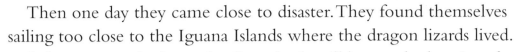

Then one day they came close to disaster. They found themselves sailing too close to the Iguana Islands where the dragon lizards lived.

"If we get much closer, the *Poppykettle* will be smashed against the rocky shore," cried one of the gnomes.

"If we get much closer, *we'll* be smashed on the shore," said another.

"If we get much closer, we'll be the dragons' lunch," said a third.

"What shall we do?" wailed a fourth.

"Blow on our sail," suggested a fifth.

"That's a silly idea!" said a sixth.

"Shut up and blow," said the seventh, and they all did.

But no matter how hard they tried to blow into the sail to make the ship leave the shore, the *Poppykettle* kept being blown inland.

As if things weren't bad enough, the tiny clay vessel caught the attention of one of the dragon lizards, which lumbered down to the rocks. Drooling at the thought of seven whole gnomes for lunch, the creature's jaw dropped and—as happens with most dragons—flames and hot air spurted out.

Fortunately for our band of travelers, the flames didn't reach them, but the hot air did. It filled their sails and blew the ship away from the shore, back out to sea. There was a lot of cheering as the *Poppykettle* was caught in a current and sailed on to safety.

The seven Inca gnomes had many more adventures in their poppykettle craft. . . . One time they were caught in a terrible storm. Day after day huge waves crashed against the *Poppykettle*, tossing it up into the air and crashing it down on the ocean . . . until the storm finally subsided.

"Phew," said one.

"That was a close call," said a second.

"I thought we were going to drown," said a third.

"There's a crack in the *Poppykettle*," said a fourth.

"There's water coming in!" added a fifth.

"Abandon ship!" cried the sixth.

"None of us can swim!" pointed out the seventh.

"Don't panic!" said a passing dolphin, tossing the *Poppykettle* –with the seven gnomes inside it–onto his back.

"We're being kidnapped!" yelped all the little gnomes at once.

"No, you're not," said the dolphin (and don't forget that El Niño ruled over all the creatures in the oceans). "I'm giving you a free ride."

The gnomes were grateful. They really were. But dolphins have a habit of jumping out of the water in graceful arches, just for the fun of it, and whenever that happened, the *Poppykettle*–with them inside it–went tumbling down the dolphin's back.

In the end they solved this problem by lashing their vessel around the dolphin's neck–or rather where a dolphin's neck would be if it had one–until they reached dry land.

"We've arrived!" shouted the gnomes, tumbling onto the sand with glee. "We've arrived!" But they had no idea where they were.

In fact, so the myth goes, El Niño's wind, waves, and sea creatures had carried the seven Inca gnomes all the way to Australia, where they lived out their days having fun!

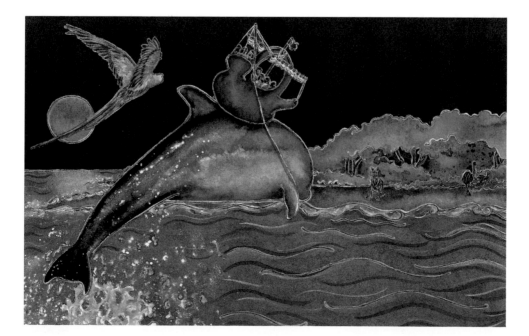

ASARE AND THE ALLIGATORS

An old Sherente myth tells of a group of seven brothers who disgraced their parents and so had to leave the safety of their village. The youngest of the brothers was Asare, and he had many adventures. This is just one of them.

"Come on, try to keep up!" said the eldest. "We've a long way to go, Asare."

"But I'm thirsty," protested the boy. They had been walking for many hours now, and his throat was dry.

"That's simple enough to solve," said the eldest. "Look." He pointed to a cluster of tucum nuts up a tree, which, like coconuts, contain a sweet liquid.

The brothers hurried to find a stick long enough to knock the nuts to the ground. They scurried here and there, and it was Asare who finally found a broken branch in the undergrowth.

"Here," he said, excitedly. He put down his hunting arrow and handed the broken piece of branch to his eldest brother.

His brother used the branch to knock the tucum nuts from the tree with a loud "THWACK," followed by another "THWACK" as they hit the ground.

The brothers hurried forward and split open the nuts to give their youngest brother a drink.

Asare drank the water from nut after nut after nut. But he was still so thirsty that they had to find another tree and knock down another cluster of nuts . . . and still his thirst wasn't quenched.

"You can't still be thirsty!" protested one of his brothers, angrily.

"But I am," cried Asare, upset that he was being shouted at.

"Don't worry," said the eldest. "There should be water just below the surface of the ground down in that hollow. We'll dig a well."

Everyone was excited by this idea. One good thing about having left the village was that there were no elders telling them what to do.

So the brothers walked down into the hollow and began to dig, first with their hands and later with sticks. Eventually there was a mighty "WHOOOOSH!" and water began spurting out of the ground.

Asare drank until he was fit to burst, and still the water poured from the ground. It formed the first river . . . which later grew into a lake and then turned into the oceans.

In the beginning, the brothers were stunned by the sight of the river. Then the eldest grinned, realizing its advantages.

"Now whenever you're thirsty, all you need to do is take a drink from those waters," he said.

But Asare wasn't smiling. "I left my arrow on the spot where I found the branch to knock down the tucum nuts," he groaned. "And that's on the other side of the water."

"Then you'll have to make yourself a new arrow," snapped another of his six brothers.

"No," said Asare. "That arrow has brought me luck when hunting."

"That's true enough," agreed the eldest. "Think of all the lizards you killed with it along the way."

Asare groaned a second time. The lizards would have been washed away by the water when the river was formed.

"The lizards may be lost," he said, which meant one less meal for the traveling brothers, "but at least I can rescue my arrow."

Before the others had time to protest, he'd jumped into the water and was making his way across to the other side. None of his brothers dared to follow him.

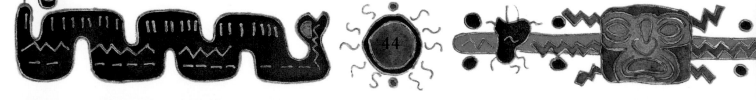

"It's too dangerous," said one.

"He could kill himself," said another.

But Asare was already scrambling up the opposite bank and scurrying back to where he'd put his favorite arrow, which, fortunately, was still on dry land.

Asare found it harder coming back the other way. For a start, he was clutching the arrow in one hand, and second, the more water that gushed from the hole he and his brothers had dug, the stronger the river's current became.

Asare made a desperate grab for a floating log that was bobbing by and released his grasp on the arrow in the process . . . only it wasn't a passing log at all—it was an alligator.

Now Asare can't be blamed for making this mistake. He had never seen an alligator before, because there had never been any alligators before—in the same way that there had been no rivers or oceans until now.

This was one of the very first alligators on earth. In fact, before the brothers had dug the hole, this alligator had been one of the lizards Asare had caught. But once it had been swept away in the water, it turned into an alligator. It did look very much like a log, except that it had mean eyes and row upon row of very sharp teeth.

"Let go of me!" demanded the alligator.

Asare did as he was told but found it hard to keep his head above water. "Let me sit on your back, Mister ugly nose," he said, "and give me a ride to the other side."

"No," said the alligator and began snapping its jaws.

This frightened Asare enough to give him a new burst of energy, and he found himself swimming through the strong current to reach the other side.

There was no sign of his brothers anywhere. They had seen Asare's arrow floating down the river and assumed that he had drowned.

Although he was on dry land once more, Asare soon discovered that his troubles weren't over. Unlike logs, not only did alligators have mean eyes and teeth but they also had legs . . . and this particular alligator was using those legs to follow Asare into the forest.

"I may have an ugly nose, but it's a big one and it will sniff you out, little human!" the alligator called out, not far behind him.

Up ahead Asare heard the "TAP-TAP" of woodpeckers pecking the bark off a tree. Asare begged for their help, and the woodpeckers covered the boy from head to toe with pieces of bark.

This not only made Asare look like a scaly monster—a bit like an upright alligator—but the bark of the tree also disguised his smell.

When the angry alligator came crashing through the undergrowth, it didn't recognize him at all. "Has a human come this way?" it asked.

"He went that way," said Asare, pointing deep into the forest, and the woodpeckers nodded their heads in agreement.

With a grunt the alligator headed off on the false trail.

Asare thanked the woodpeckers, threw off his disguise, and made his way back to the river. He'd only been in the water a few moments when he came face to face with another alligator. He didn't even consider asking this one to carry him across the river. He tried to swim around it, but it gave chase.

Again Asare found himself heading for the forest and thought he could hear voices up ahead. Was this the sound of his brothers? Had they crossed the river to rescue him? Was he safe at last? His brothers had arrows and could frighten the alligator. But no—it was a group of monkeys, busy eating fruit and chattering about the day's events.

"Please hide me," said the boy. "I'm being chased by a creature from the river, and it has plenty of teeth."

When the monkeys saw Asare, they grew quiet and stared.

One of them pointed to the skins of the jatoba fruit they were eating, which were heaped in a big pile in front of them.

Asare had barely had time to wriggle under the pile and hide when the second alligator appeared in the clearing.

"Have you seen a boy?" it asked.

"You're a funny-looking creature," said one of the monkeys, who couldn't help commenting on the alligator's appearance.

"I've seen lots of boys," said another.

"In fact—" began the third monkey, about to tell the alligator about Asare hiding under the jatoba skins, because most monkeys are terrible at keeping secrets. They just can't help it.

Fortunately for Asare another monkey hit the talkative monkey on the lips before it could give the game away, and the alligator made off into the undergrowth.

Thanking the monkeys, Asare came out from his hiding place and swam across the river. At long last he caught up with his brothers, who were amazed and delighted that he was still alive.

Together they bathed in the newly formed ocean. They became so clean and shiny that they now gleam in the sky as seven stars, called the Seven Brothers.

MYTHS AND LEGENDS RESOURCES

Here is just a sampling of other resources to look for. These resources on myths and legends are broken down into groups. Enjoy!

GENERAL MYTHOLOGY

The Children's Dictionary of Mythology *edited by David Leeming* (Franklin Watts, 1999). This volume is a dictionary of terms, names, and places in the mythology of various cultures around the world.

Creation Read-aloud Stories from Many Lands *retold by Ann Pilling* (Candlewick Press, 1997). This is a collection of sixteen stories retold in an easy style and presented in three general groups: beginnings, warmth and light, and animals.

The Crystal Pool: Myths and Legends of the World *by Geraldine McCaughrean* (Margaret K. McElderry Books, 1998). Twenty-eight myths and legends from around the world comprise this book. They include the Chinese legend "The Alchemist" and the Celtic legend "Culloch and the Big Pig."

Encyclopedia Mythica
http://www.pantheon.org/areas/mythology/
From this page of the *Encyclopedia Mythica* site you can select from any of five countries to have the mythology of that area displayed.

A Family Treasury of Myths from Around the World *retold by Viviane Koenig* (Abrams, 1998). This collection of ten stories includes myths from Egypt, Africa, Greece, and other places around the world.

Goddesses, Heroes and Shamans: The Young People's Guide to World Mythology *edited by Cynthia O'Neill and others* (Kingfisher, 1994). This book introduces the reader to over five hundred mythological characters from around the world.

Gods, Goddesses and Monsters: An Encyclopedia of World Mythology *retold by Sheila Keenan* (Scholastic, 2000). This beautifully illustrated book discusses the characters and themes of the myths of peoples from Asia to Africa, to North and South America.

The Golden Hoard: Myths and Legends of the World *retold by Geraldine McCaughrean* (Margaret K. McElderry Books, 1995). This book contains twenty-two myths and legends that are exciting, adventurous, magical, and poetic.

The Illustrated Book of Myths: Tales and Legends of the World *retold by Neil Philips* (Dorling Kindersley, 1995). This beautifully illustrated collection brings together many of the most popular of the Greek and Roman, Norse, Celtic, Egyptian, Native American, African, and Indian myths.

Kids Zone: Myths and Fables from Around the World
http://www.afroam.org/children/myths/myths.html
Just click on your choice of the sixteen stories listed, and it will appear in full text.

Legends http://www.planetozkids.com/oban/legends.htm
From this Web page you can get the full text of any of the many listings.

Mythical Birds and Beasts from Many Lands *retold by Margaret Mayo* (Dutton, 1996). This book is a collection of stories that illustrate the special powers of birds and beasts that have become a part of folklore around the world.

Mythology *by Neil Philip* (Alfred A. Knopf, 1999). This superbly illustrated volume from the "Eyewitness Books" series surveys the treatment of such topics as gods and goddesses, the heavens, creation, the elements, and evil as expressed in various mythologies around the world.

Mythology *CD-ROM for Mac and Windows* (Thomas S. Klise, 1996). Educational games and puzzles, a glossary, and a testing section are all part of this CD introduction to Greek and Roman mythology.

Myths and Legends *by Neil Philip* (DK Publishing, 1999). More than fifty myths and legends from around the world are explained through works of art, text, and annotation by one of the world's foremost experts on mythology and folklore.

The New York Public Library Amazing Mythology: A Book of Answers for Kids *by Brendan January* (John Wiley, 2000). Over two hundred questions and answers introduce myths from many ancient cultures, including Egyptian, Greek, Roman, Celtic, Norse, and Native American.

Plays from Mythology: Grades 4-6 *by L.E. McCullough* (Smith and Kraus, 1998). Twelve original plays are included, each with suggestions for staging and costumes.

Sources for Mythology
http://www.best.com/~atta/mythsrcs.html
In addition to defining mythology and distinguishing it from legend and folklore, this Web site lists primary sources for myths from many regions of the world, as well as magazines, dictionaries, and other resources relating to mythology.

Sun, Moon and Stars *retold by Mary Hoffman* (Dutton, 1998). More than twenty myths and legends from around the world, all explaining what was seen in the sky, make up this exquisitely illustrated book.

AFRICAN

African Gods and their Associates
http://www3.sympatico.ca/untangle/africang.html
This Web page gives you a list of the African gods with links to further information about them.

African Myths
http://www.cybercomm.net/~grandpa/africanmyths.html
Full text of several tales from the Kenya, Hausa, Ashanti, and Nyanja tribes are included in this Web site.

Anansi and the Talking Melon *retold by Eric A. Kimmel* (Holiday House, 1994). Anansi, a legendary character from Africa, tricks Elephant and some other animals into thinking that the melon in which he is hiding can talk.

Children's Stories from Africa *4 Video recordings (VHS)* (Monterey Home Video, 1997). Among the African Legends on this page: "How the Hare Got His Long Legs," "How the Porcupine Got His Quills," "The Brave Sititunga," and "The Greedy Spider."

The Hero with an African Face: Mythic Wisdom of Traditional Africa *by Clyde W. Ford* (Bantam, 2000). "The Hero with an African Face" is only one of the several stories included in this book, which also includes a map of the peoples and myths of Africa and a pronunciation guide for African words.

Kings, Gods and Spirits from African Mythology *retold by Jan Knappert* (Peter Bedrick Books, 1993). This illustrated collection contains myths and legends of the peoples of Africa.

Legends of Africa *by Mwizenge Tembo* (Metro Books, 1996). This indexed and illustrated volume is from the "Myths of the World" series.

Myths and Legends *retold by O. B. Duane* (Brockhampton Press, 1998). Duane has vividly retold some of the most gripping African tales.

CELTIC

Celtic Myths *retold by Sam McBratney* (Peter Bedrick, 1997). This collection of fifteen illustrated stories draws from English, Irish, Scottish, and Welsh folklore.

Excalibur *retold by Hudson Talbott* (Books of Wonder, 1996). In this illustrated story from the legends of King Arthur, Arthur receives his magical sword, Excalibur

Irish Fairy Tales and Legends *retold by Una Leavy* (Robert Rinehart, 1996). Cuchulainn, Deirdre, and Fionn Mac Cumhail are only three of the legendary characters you will meet in this volume.

Irish Myths and Legends
http://www.mc.maricopa.edu/users/shoemaker/
   Celtic/index.html
This Web site is for those more serious in their study of Irish myths and legends.

King Arthur *by Rosalind Kerven* (DK Publishing, 1998). This book from the "Eyewitness Classic" series is a retelling of the boy who was fated to be the "Once and Future King" It includes illustrated notes to explain the historical background of the story.

Robin Hood and His Merry Men *retold by Jane Louise Curry* (Margaret K. McElderry, 1994). This collection contains seven short stories of the legendary hero Robin Hood, who lived with his band of followers in Sherwood Forest.

The World of King Arthur and his Court: People, Places, Legend and Love *by Kevin Crossley-Holland* (Dutton, 1998). The author combines legend, anecdote, fact, and speculation to help answer some of the questions regarding King Arthur and his chivalrous world.

CHINESE

Asian Mythology *by Rachel Storm* (Lorenz, 2000). Included in this volume are myths and legends of China.

Chinese Culture
http://chineseculture.about.com/culture/
   chineseculture/msub82.htm
Use this Web page as a starting point for further exploration about Chinese myths and legends.

Chinese Mythology by *Anne Birrell* (Johns Hopkins, 1999). This comprehensive introduction to Chinese mythology will meet the needs of the more serious and the general reader

Chinese Myths and Legends *retold by O. B. Duane and others* (Brockhampton Press, 1998). Introductory notes by the author give further explanation of the thirty-eight stories included in this illustrated volume.

Dragons and Demons by *Stewart Ross* (Cooper Beech, 1998). Included in this collection of myths and legends from Asia are the Chinese myths "Chang Lung the Dragon" and "The Ugly Scholar."

Dragons, Gods and Spirits from Chinese Mythology *retold by Tao Tao Liu Sanders* (Peter Bedrick Books, 1994). The stories in this book include ancient myths about nature, the gods, and creation as well as religious legends.

Fa Mulan: The Story of a Woman Warrior *retold by Robert D. San Souci* (Hyperion, 1998). Artists Jean and Mou-Sien Tseng illustrate this Chinese legend of a young heroine who is courageous, selfless, and wise.

Land of the Dragon: Chinese Myth by *Tony Allan* (Time-Life, 1999). This volume from the "Myth and Mankind" series includes many of China's myths as well as examination of the myth and its historical roots.

Selected Chinese Myths and Fantasies
http://www.chinavista.com/experience/story/story.html
From this Web site and its links you will find several Chinese myths that are enjoyed by children as well as the history of Chinese mythology.

EGYPTIAN

Egyptian Gods and Goddesses by *Henry Barker* (Grosset and Dunlap, 1999). In this book designed for the young reader, religious beliefs of ancient Egypt are discussed, as well as their gods and goddesses.

Egyptian Mythology A-Z: A Young Reader's Companion by *Pat Remler* (Facts on File, 2000). Alphabetically arranged, this resource defines words relating to Egyptian mythology.

Egyptian Myths *retold by Jacqueline Morley* (Peter Bedrick Books, 1999). Legends of the pharaohs, myths about creation, and the search for the secret of all knowledge, make up this illustrated book.

The Gods and Goddesses of Ancient Egypt by *Leonard Everett Fisher* (Holiday House, 1997). This artist/writer describes thirteen of the most important Egyptian gods.

Gods and Myths of Ancient Egypt by *Mary Barnett* (Regency House, 1996). Beautiful color photographs are used to further explain the text in this summary of Egyptian mythology.

Gods and Pharaohs from Egyptian Mythology *retold by Geraldine Harris* (Peter Bedrick Books, 1992). The author gives some background information about the Ancient Egyptians and then retells more than twenty of their myths.

Myth Man's Egyptian Homework Help
http://egyptmyth.com/
Cool Facts and Fun for Kids and *Egyptian Myth Encyclopedia* are only two of the many wonderful links this page will lead you to.

Myths and Civilizations of the Ancient Egyptians by *Sarah Quie* (Peter Bedrick Books, 1998). The author intersperses Egypt's myths with a history of its civilization in this illustrated volume.

The Secret Name of Ra *retold by Anne Rowe* (Rigby Interactive Library, 1996). In this Egyptian myth, Isis tricks Ra into revealing his secret name so that she and her husband Osiris can become rulers of the earth.

Tales from Ancient Egypt *retold by George Hart* (Hoopoe Books, 1994). The seven tales in this collection include stories of animals, of Isis and Horus, of a sailor lost on a magic island, and of pharaohs and their magicians.

Who's Who in Egyptian Mythology by *Anthony S. Mercatante* (Scarecrow Press, 1995). The author has compiled a concise, easy-to-use dictionary of ancient Egyptian deities.

GREEK

Allta and the Queen: A Tale of Ancient Greece by *Priscilla Galloway* (Annick Press, 1995). This made-up story, which is based on Homer's epic poem, *The Odyssey*, reads like a novel.

Cupid and Psyche *retold by M. Charlotte Craft* (Morrow Junior Books, 1996). This classic love story from Greek mythology will appeal to young and old.

Gods and Goddesses by *John Malam* (Peter Bedrick Books, 1999). This volume is packed with information about the important gods and goddesses of ancient Greece, including Zeus, Hera, Athena, and Hades.

Greek and Roman Mythology by *Dan Nardo* (Lucent, 1998). The author examines the historical development of Greco-Roman mythology, its heroes, and its influence on the history of Western civilization.

Guide for Using D'Aulaires' Book of Greek Myths in the Classroom *by Cynthia Ross* (Teacher Created Materials, 1993). This reproducible book includes sample plans, author information, vocabulary-building ideas, cross-curricular activities, quizzes, and many ideas for extending this classic work.

Hercules *by Robert Burleigh* (Harcourt Brace, 1999). Watercolor and color pencil illustrations help to tell the story of Hercules's final labor in which he went back to the underworld and brought back the three-headed dog, Cerberus.

Medusa *by Deborah Nourse Lattimire* (Joanna Cotler Books, 2000). The author/illustrator of this book re-creates the tragedy of one of the best-known Greek myths, the tale of the beautiful Medussa whose conceit causes a curse be placed on her.

The Myths and Legends of Ancient Greece *CD-ROM for Mac and Windows* (Clearvue, 1996). This CD conveys the heroic ideals and spirit of Greek mythology as it follows ten of the best-known myths.

Mythweb http://www.mythweb.com/
This Web page provides links to Greek gods, heroes, an encyclopedia of mythology, and teacher resources.

Pegasus, the Flying Horse *retold by Jane Yolen* (Dutton, 1998). This Greek myth tells of how Bellerophon, with the help of Athena, tames the winged horse Pegasus and conquers the monstrous Chimaera.

The Race of the Golden Apples *retold by Claire Martin* (Dial, 1991). Caldecott Medal winners Leo and Diane Dillon have illustrated this myth of Atalanta, the beautiful Greek princess.

The Random House Book of Greek Myths *by Joan D. Vinge* (Random House, 1999). The author retells some of the famous Greek myths about gods, goddesses, humans, heroes, and monsters, explaining the background of the tales and why these tales have survived.

The Robber Baby: Stories from the Greek Myths *retold by Anne Rockwell* (Greenwillow Books, 1994). Anne Rockwell, a well-known name in children's literature, has put together a superbly retold collection of myths that will be enjoyed by readers of all ages.

NORSE

Beowulf *by Welwyn Wilton Katz* (Groundwood, 2000). The illustrations in this classic legend are based on the art of the Vikings.

Favorite Norse Myths *retold by Mary Pope Osborne* (Scholastic, 1996). These fourteen tales of Norse gods, goddesses, and giants are based on the oldest written sources of Norse mythology, *Prose Edda* and *Poetic Edda*.

The Giant King *by Rosalind Kerven* (NTC Publishing Group, 1998). Photos of artifacts from the Viking Age illustrate these two stories that are rooted in Norse mythology.

Gods and Heroes from Viking Mythology *by Brian Branston* (Peter Bedrick Books, 1994). This illustrated volume tells the stories of Thor, Balder, King Gylfi, and other Nordic gods and goddesses

Handbook of Norse Mythology *by John Lindow* (Ambcc, 2001). For the advanced reader, this handbook covers the tales, their literary and oral sources, includes an A-to-Z of the key mythological figures, concepts and events, and so much more.

Kids Domain Fact File
http://www.kidsdomain.co.uk/teachers/resources/
  fact_file_viking_gods_and_goddesses.html
This child-centered Web page is a dictionary of Viking gods and goddesses.

Myths and Civilization of the Vikings *by Hazel Martell* (Peter Bedrick, 1998). Each of the nine stories in this book is followed by a non-fiction spread with information about Viking society.

Norse Mythology: The Myths and Legends of the Nordic Gods *retold by Arthur Cotterell* (Lorenz Books, 2000). This encyclopedia of the Nordic peoples' myths and legends is generously illustrated with fine art paintings of the classic stories.

Odins' Family: Myths of the Vikings *retold by Neil Philip* (Orchard Books, 1996). This collection of stories of Odin, the All-father, and the other Viking gods Thor, Tyr, Frigg, and Loer is full of excitement that encompasses both tragedy and comedy.

Stolen Thunder: A Norse Myth *retold by Shirley Climo* (Houghton Mifflin, 1994). This story, beautifully illustrated by Alexander Koshkin, retells the Norse myth about the god of Thunder and the recovery of his magic hammer Mjolnir, from the Frost Giany, Thrym.

North American

Buffalo Dance: A Blackfoot Legend *retold by Nancy Can Laan* (Little, Brown and Company, 1993). This illustrated version of the Native North American legend tells of the ritual performed before the buffalo hunt.

The Favorite Uncle Remus *by Joel Chandler Harris* (Houghton Mifflin, 1948). This classic work of literature is a collection of stories about Brer Rabbit, Brer Fox, Brer Tarrypin, and others that were told to the author as he grew up in the South.

Iktomi Loses his Eyes: A Plains Indian Story *retold by Paul Goble* (Orchard Books, 1999). The legendary character Iktomi finds himself in a predicament after losing his eyes when he misuses a magical trick.

The Legend of John Henry *retold by Terry Small* (Doubleday, 1994). This African American legendary character, a steel driver on the railroad, pits his strength and speed against the new steam engine hammer that is putting men out of jobs.

The Legend of the White Buffalo Woman *retold by Paul Goble* (National Geographic Society, 1998). This Native American Plains legend tells the story of the White Buffalo Woman who gave her people the Sacred Calf Pipe so that people would pray and commune with the Great Spirit.

Myths and Legends for American Indian Youth
http://www.kstrom.net/isk/stories/myths.html
Stories from Native Americans across the United States are included in these pages.

Snail Girl Brings Water: a Navajo Story *retold by Geri Keams* (Rising Moon, 1998). This retelling of a traditional Navajo re-creation myth explains how water came to earth.

The Woman Who Fell from the Sky: The Iroquois Story of Creation *retold by John Bierhirst* (William Morrow, 1993). This myth describes how the creation of the world was begun by a woman who fell down to earth from the sky country, and how it was finished by her two sons.

South American (including Central American)

Gods and Goddesses of the Ancient Maya *by Leonard Everett Fisher* (Holiday House, 1999). With text and illustration inspired by the art, glyphs, and sculpture of the ancient Maya, this artist and author describes twelve of the most important Maya gods.

How Music Came to the World: An Ancient Mexican Myth *retold by Hal Ober* (Houghton Mifflin, 1994). This illustrated book, which includes author notes and a pronunciation guide, is an Aztec pourquoi story that explains how music came to the world.

Llama and the Great Flood *retold by Ellen Alexander* (Thomas Y. Crowell, 1989). In this illustrated retelling of the Peruvian myth about the Great Flood, a llama warns his master of the coming destruction and leads him and his family to refuge on a high peak in the Andes.

The Legend of the Poinsettia *retold by Tomie dePaola* (G. P. Putnam's Sons,1994). This beautifully illustrated Mexican legend tells of how the poinsettia came to be when a young girl offered her gift to the Christ child.

Lost Realms of Gold: South American Myth *edited by Tony Allan* (Time-Life Books, 2000). This volume, which captures the South American mythmakers' fascination with magic, includes the tale of the first Inca who built the city of Cuzco, as well as the story of the sky people who discovered the rain forest.

People of Corn: A Mayan Story *retold by Mary-Joan Gerson* (Little, Brown, 1995). In this richly illustrated creation story, the gods first try and fail, then try and fail again before they finally succeed.

Tales from the Rain Forest: Myths and Legends from the Amazonian Indians of Brazil *retold by Mercedes Dorson* (Ecco Press, 1997). Ten stories from this region include "The Origin of Rain" and "How the Stars Came to Be."

WHO'S WHO IN MYTHS AND LEGENDS

This is a cumulative listing of some important characters found in all eight volumes of the **World Book Myths and Legends** series.

A

Aegir (EE jihr), also called Hler, was the god of the sea and the husband of Ran in Norse myths. He was lord of the undersea world where drowned sailors spent their days.

Amma (ahm mah) was the creator of the world in the myths of the Dogon people of Africa. Mother Earth was his wife, and Water and Light were his children. Amma also created the people of the world.

Amun (AH muhn), later Amun-Ra, became the king of gods in later Egyptian myths. Still later he was seen as another form of Ra.

Anubis (uh NOO bihs) in ancient Egypt was the god of the dead and helper to Osiris. He had the head of a jackal.

Ao (ow) was a giant turtle in a Chinese myth. He saved the life of Kui.

Aphrodite (af ruh DY tee) in ancient Greece was the goddess of love. She was known for her beauty. The Romans called her Venus.

Arianrod (air YAN rohd) in Welsh legends was the mother of the hero Llew.

Arthur (AHR thur) in ancient Britain was the king of the Britons. He probably was a real person who ruled long before the age of knights in armor. His queen was Guinevere.

Athena (uh THEE nuh) in ancient Greece was the goddess of war. The Romans called her Minerva.

Atum (AH tuhm) was the creator god of ancient Egypt and the father of Shu and Tefnut. He later became Ra-Atum.

B

Babe (bayb) in North American myths was the big blue ox owned by Paul Bunyan.

Balder (BAWL dur) was the god of light in Norse myths. He was the most handsome of all gods and was Frigga's favorite son.

Balor (BAL awr) was an ancient chieftain in Celtic myths who had an evil eye. He fought Lug, the High King of Ireland.

Ban Hu (bahn hoo) was the dog god in a myth that tells how the Year of the Dog in the Chinese calendar got its name.

Bastet (BAS teht), sometimes Bast (bast) in ancient Egypt was the mother goddess. She was often shown as a cat. Bastet was the daughter of Ra and the sister of Hathor and Sekhmet.

Bellerophon (buh LEHR uh fahn) in ancient Greek myths was a hero who captured and rode the winged horse, Pegasus.

Blodeuwedd was the wife of Llew in Welsh legends. She was made of flowers woven together by magic.

Botoque (boh toh kay) in Kayapó myths was the boy who first ate cooked meat and told people about fire.

Brer Rabbit (brair RAB iht) was a clever trickster rabbit in North American myths.

C

Chameleon (kuh MEEL yuhn) in a Yoruba myth of Africa was a messenger sent to trick the god Olokun and teach him a lesson.

Conchobar (KAHN koh bahr), also called Conor, was the king of Ulster. He was a villain in many Irish myths.

Coyote (ky OH tee) was an evil god in myths of the Maidu and some other Native American people.

Crow (kroh) in Inuit myths was the wise bird who brought daylight to the Inuit people.

Cuchulain (koo KUHL ihn), also Cuchullain or Cuchulan, in Irish myths was Ireland's greatest warrior of all time. He was the son of Lug and Dechtire.

Culan (KOO luhn) in Irish myths was a blacksmith. His hound was killed by Setanta, who later became Cuchulain.

D

Davy Crockett (DAY vee KRAHK iht) was a real person. He is remembered as an American frontier hero who died in battle and also in legends as a great hunter and woodsman.

Dechtire (DEHK teer) in Irish myths was the sister of King Conchobar and mother of Cuchulain.

Deirdre (DAIR dray) in Irish myths was the daughter of Fedlimid. She refused to wed Conchobar. It was said that she would lead to Ireland's ruin.

Di Jun (dee joon) was god of the Eastern Sky in Chinese myths. He lived in a giant mulberry tree.

Di Zang Wang (dee zahng wahng) in Chinese myths was a Buddhist monk who was given that name when he became the lord of the underworld. His helper was Yan Wang, god of the dead.

Dionysus (dy uh NY suhs) was the god of wine in ancient Greek myths. He carried a staff wrapped in vines.

Dolapo was the wife of Kigbo in a Yoruba myth of Africa.

E

Eight Immortals (ihm MAWR tuhlz) in Chinese myths were eight ordinary human beings whose good deeds led them to truth and enlightenment. The Eight Immortals were godlike heroes. They had special powers to help people.

El Niño (ehl NEEN yoh) in Inca myths was the ruler of the wind, the weather, and the ocean and its creatures.

Emer (AYV ur) in Irish myths was the daughter of Forgal the Wily and wife of Cuchulain.

F

Fafnir (FAHV nihr) in Norse myths was a son of Hreidmar. He killed his father for his treasure, sent his brother Regin away, and turned himself into a dragon.

Frey (fray), also called Freyr, was the god of summer in Norse myths. His chariot was pulled by a huge wild boar.

Freya (FRAY uh) was the goddess of beauty and love in Norse myths. Her chariot was pulled by two large cats.

Frigga (FRIHG uh), also called Frigg, in Norse myths was the wife of Odin and mother of many gods. She was the most powerful goddess in Asgard.

Frog was an animal prince in an Alur myth of Africa. He and his brother, Lizard, competed for the right to inherit the throne of their father.

Fu Xi (foo shee) in a Chinese myth was a boy who, with his sister Nü Wa, freed the Thunder God and was rewarded. His name means Gourd Boy.

G

Gaunab was Death, who took on a human form in a Khoi myth of Africa. Tsui'goab fought with Gaunab to save his people.

Geb (gehb) in ancient Egypt was the Earth itself. All plants and trees grew from his back. He was the brother and husband of Nut and the father of the gods Osiris, Isis, Seth, and Nephthys.

Glooscap (glohs kap) was a brave and cunning god in the myths of Algonquian Native American people. He was a trickster who sometimes got tricked.

Guinevere (GWIHN uh vihr) in British and Welsh legends was King Arthur's queen, who was also loved by Sir Lancelot.

Gwydion (GWIHD ih uhn) in Welsh legends was the father of Llew and the nephew of the magician and ruler, Math.

H

Hades (HAY deez) in ancient Greece was the god of the dead. Hades was also called Pluto (PLOO toh). The Romans called him Dis.

Hairy Man was a frightening monster in African American folk tales.

Harpy (HAHRP ee) was one of the hideous winged women in Greek myths. The hero Jason and his Argonauts freed King Phineas from the harpies' power.

Hathor (HATH awr) was worshiped in the form of a cow in ancient Egypt, but she also appeared as an angry lioness. She was the daughter of Ra and the sister of Bastet and Sekhmet.

Heimdall (HAYM dahl) was the god in Norse myths who guarded the rainbow bridge joining Asgard, the home of the gods, to other worlds.

Hel (hehl), also called Hela, was the goddess of death in Norse myths. The lower half of her body was like a rotting corpse. Hel was Loki's daughter.

Helen (HEHL uhn), called Helen of Troy, was a real person in ancient Greece. According to legend, she was known as the most beautiful woman in the world. Her capture by Paris led to the Trojan War.

Heng E (huhng ay), sometimes called Chang E, was a woman in Chinese myths who became the moon goddess. She was the wife of Yi the Archer.

Hera (HEHR uh) in ancient Greece was the queen of heaven and the wife of Zeus. The Romans called her Juno.

Heracles (HEHR uh kleez) in ancient Greek myths was a hero of great strength. He was the son of Zeus. He had to complete twelve tremendous tasks in order to become one of the gods. The Romans called him Hercules.

Hermes (HUR meez) was the messenger of the gods in Greek myths. He wore winged sandals. The Romans called him Mercury.

Hoder (HOO dur) was Balder's twin brother in Norse myths. He was blind. It was said that after a mighty battle he and Balder would be born again.

Hoenir (HAY nihr), also called Honir, was a god in Norse myths. In some early myths, he is said to be Odin's brother.

Horus (HAWR uhs) in ancient Egypt was the son of Isis and Osiris. He was often shown with the head of a falcon. Horus fought Seth to rule Egypt.

Hreidmar (HRAYD mahr) was a dwarf king in Norse myths who held Odin for a huge pile of treasure. His sons were Otter, Fafnir, and Regin.

Hyrrokkin (HEER rahk kihn) in Norse myths was a terrifying female giant who rode an enormous wolf using poisonous snakes for reins.

I

Irin-Mage (eereen mah geh) in Tupinambá myths was the only person to be saved when the creator, Monan, destroyed the other humans. Irin-Mage became the ancestor of all people living today.

Isis (EYE sihs) in ancient Egypt was the goddess of fertility and a master of magic. She became the most powerful of all the gods and goddesses. She was the sister and wife of Osiris and mother of Horus.

J

Jade Emperor (jayd EHM puhr uhr) in Buddhist myths of China was the chief god in Heaven.

Jason (JAY suhn) was a hero in Greek myths. His ship was the Argo, and the men who sailed with him on his adventures were called the Argonauts.

Johnny Appleseed (AP uhl seed) was a real person, John Chapman. He is remembered in legends as the person who traveled across North America, planting apple orchards.

K

Kaboi (kah boy) was a very wise man in a Carajá myth. He helped his people find their way from their underground home to the surface of the earth.

Kewawkwuí (kay wow kwoo) were a group of powerful, frightening giants and magicians in the myths of Algonquian Native American people.

Kigbo (keeg boh) was a stubborn man in a Yoruba myth of Africa. His stubbornness got him into trouble with spirits.

Kodoyanpe (koh doh yahn pay) was a good god in the myths of the Maidu and some other Native American people. He was the brother of the evil god Coyote.

Kuang Zi Lian (kwahng dsee lee ehn) in a Taoist myth of China was a very rich, greedy farmer who was punished by one of the Eight Immortals.

Kui in Chinese myths was an ugly, brilliant scholar who became God of Examinations.

Kvasir (KVAH sihr) in Norse myths was the wisest of all the gods in Asgard.

L

Lancelot (lan suh laht) in British and Welsh legends was King Arthur's friend and greatest knight. He was secretly in love with Guinevere.

Lao Zi (low dzuh) was the man who founded the Chinese religion of Taoism. He wrote down the Taoist beliefs in a book, the *Tao Te Ching*.

Li Xuan (lee shwahn) was one of the Eight Immortals in ancient Chinese myths.

Light (lyt) was a child of Amma, the creator of the world, in a myth of the Dogon people of Africa.

Lizard (LIHZ urd) was an animal prince in an Alur myth of Africa. He was certain that he, and not his brother, Frog, would inherit the throne of their father.

Llew Llaw Gyffes (LE yoo HLA yoo GUHF ehs), also Lleu Law Gyffes, was a hero in Welsh myths who had many adventures. His mother was Arianrod and his father was Gwydion.

Loki (LOH kee) in Norse myths was a master trickster. His friends were Odin and Thor. Loki was half giant and half god, and could be funny and also cruel. He caused the death of Balder.

Lord of Heaven was the chief god in some ancient Chinese myths.

Lug (luk) in Irish myths was the Immortal High King of Ireland, Master of All Arts.

M

Maira-Monan (mah ee rah moh nahn) was the most powerful son of Irin-Mage in Tupinambá myths. He was destroyed by people who were afraid of his powers.

Manco Capac (mahn kih kah pahk) in Inca myths was the founder of the Inca people. He was one of four brothers and four sisters who led the Inca to their homeland.

Manitou (MAN ih toh) was the greatest and most powerful of all gods in Native American myths of the Iroquois people.

Math (mohth) in Welsh myths was a magician who ruled the Welsh kingdom of Gwynedd.

Michabo (mee chah boh) in the myths of Algonquian Native American people was the Great Hare, who taught people to hunt and brought them luck. He was a son of West Wind.

Monan (moh nahn) was the creator in Tupinambá myths.

Monkey (MUNG kee) is the hero of many Chinese stories. The most cunning of all monkeys, he became the king of monkeys and caused great troubles for the gods.

N

Nanook (na NOOK) was the white bear in myths of the Inuit people.

Naoise (NEE see) in Irish myths was Conchobar's nephew and the lover of Deirdre. He was the son of Usnech and brother of Ardan and Ainle.

Nekumonta (neh koo mohn tah) in Native American myths of the Iroquois people was a person whose goodness helped him save his people from a terrible sickness.

Nü Wa (nyuh wah) in a Chinese myth was a girl who, with her brother, Fu Xi, freed the Thunder God and was rewarded. Her name means Gourd Girl.

Nuada (NOO uh thuh) in Irish myths was King of the Tuatha Dé Danann, the rulers of all Ireland. He had a silver hand.

O

Odin (OH dihn), also called Woden, in Norse myths was the chief of all the gods and a brave warrior. He had only one eye. He was the husband of Frigga and father of many of the gods. His two advisers were the ravens Hugin and Munin.

Odysseus (oh DIHS ee uhs) was a Greek hero who fought in the Trojan War. The poet Homer wrote of his many adventures.

Oedipus (ED uh puhs) was a tragic hero in Greek myths. He unknowingly killed his own father and married his mother.

Olodumare (oh loh doo mah ray) was the supreme god in Yoruba myths of Africa.

Olokun (oh loh koon) was the god of water and giver of life in Yoruba myths of Africa. He challenged Olodumare for the right to rule.

Orpheus (AWR fee uhs) in Greek myths was famed for his music. He followed his wife, Euridice, to the kingdom of the dead to plead for her life.

Osiris (oh SY rihs) in ancient Egypt was the ruler of the dead in the kingdom of the West. He was the brother and husband of Isis and the father of Horus.

P

Pamola (pah moh lah) in the myths of Algonquian Native American people was an evil spirit of the night.

Pan Gu (pahn goo) in Chinese myths was the giant who was the first living being.

Pandora (pan DAWR uh) in ancient Greek myths was the first woman.

Paris (PAR ihs) was a real person, a hero from the city of Troy. He captured Helen, the queen of a Greek kingdom, and took her to Troy.

Paul Bunyan (pawl BUHN yuhn) was a tremendously strong giant lumberjack in North American myths.

Perseus (PUR see uhs) was a human hero in myths of ancient Greece. His most famous adventure was killing Medusa, a creature who turned anyone who looked at her to stone.

Poseidon (puh SY duhn) was the god of the sea in myths of ancient Greece. He carried a three-pronged spear called a trident to make storms and control the waves. The Romans called him Neptune.

Prometheus (pruh MEE thee uhs) was the cleverest of the gods in Greek myths. He was a friend to humankind.

Q

Queen Mother of the West was a goddess in Chinese myths.

R

Ra (rah), sometimes Re (ray), was the sun god of ancient Egypt. He was often shown with the head of a hawk. Re became the most important god. Other gods were sometimes combined with him and had Ra added to their names.

Ran (rahn) was the goddess of the sea in Norse myths. She pulled sailors from their boats in a large net and dragged them underwater.

Red Jacket in Chinese myths was an assistant to Wen Chang, the god of literature. His job was to help students who hadn't worked very hard.

S

Sekhmet (SEHK meht) in ancient Egypt was a blood-thirsty goddess with the head of a lioness. She was the daughter of Ra and the sister of Bastet and Hathor.

Setanta in Irish myths was Cuchulain's name before he killed the hound of Culan.

Seth (set), sometimes Set, in ancient Egypt was the god of chaos and confusion, who fought Horus to rule Egypt. He was the evil son of Geb and Nut.

Shanewis (shah nay wihs) in Native American myths of the Iroquois people was the wife of Nekumonta.

Shu (shoo) in ancient Egypt was the father of the sky goddess Nut. He held Nut above Geb, the Earth, to keep the two apart.

Sinchi Roca was the second emperor of the Inca. According to legend, he was the son of Ayar Manco (later known as Manco Capac) and his sister Mama Ocllo.

Skirnir (SKEER nihr) in Norse myths was a brave, faithful servant of the god Frey.

Sphinx (sfihngks) in Greek myths was a creature that was half lion and half woman, with eagle wings. It killed anyone who failed to answer its riddle.

T

Tefnut (TEHF noot) was the moon goddess in ancient Egypt. She was the sister and wife of Shu and the mother of Nut and Geb.

Theseus (THEE see uhs) was a human hero in myths of ancient Greece. He killed the Minotaur, a half-human, half-bull creature, and freed its victims.

Thor (thawr) was the god of thunder in Norse myths. He crossed the skies in a chariot pulled by goats and had a hammer, Mjollnir, and a belt, Meginjardir.

Thunder God (THUN dur gahd) in Chinese myths was the god of thunder and rain. He got his power from water and was powerless if he could not drink.

Tsui'goab (tsoo ee goh ahb) was the god of rain in myths of the Khoi people of Africa. He was a human who became a god after he fought to save his people.

Tupan (too pahn) was the spirit of thunder and lightning in Inca myths.

Tyr (tihr) was the god of war in Norse myths. He was the bravest god and was honorable and true, as well. He had just one hand.

U

Utgard-Loki (OOT gahrd LOH kee) in Norse myths was the clever, crafty giant king of Utgard. He once disguised himself as a giant called Skrymir to teach Thor a lesson.

W

Water God (WAW tur gahd) in Chinese myths was a god who sent rain and caused floods.

Wen Chang (wehn chuhng) in Chinese myths was the god of literature. His assistants were Kui and Red Jacket.

Wu (woo) was a lowly courtier in a Chinese myth who fell in love with a princess.

X

Xi He (shee heh) in Chinese myths was the goddess wife of Di Jun, the god of the eastern sky.

Xiwangmu (shee wahng moo) in Chinese myths was the owner of the Garden of Immortal Peaches.

Xuan Zang (shwahn dsahng), also called Tripitaka, was a real person, a Chinese Buddhist monk who traveled to India to gather copies of religious writings. Legends about him tell that Monkey was his traveling companion.

Y

Yan Wang (yahn wahng) was the god of the dead and judge of the first court of the Underworld in Chinese myths. He was helper to Di Zang Wang.

Yao (yow) was a virtuous emperor in Chinese myths. Because Yao lived simply and was a good leader, Yi the Archer was sent to help him.

Yi (yee) was an archer in Chinese myths who was sent by Di Jun to save the earth, in answer to Yao's prayers.

Z

Zeus (zoos) in ancient Greece was the king of gods and the god of thunder and lightning. The Romans called him Jupiter.

Zhao Shen Xiao (zhow shehn shi ow) in Chinese myths was a good magistrate, or official, who arrested the greedy merchant Kuang Zi Lian.

Myths and Legends Glossary

This is a cumulative glossary of some important places and terms found in all eight volumes of the **World Book Myths and Legends** series.

A

Alfheim (AHLF hym) in Norse myth was the home of the light elves.

Asgard (AS gahrd) in Norse myths was the home of the warrior gods who were called the Aesir. It was connected to the earth by a rainbow bridge.

Augean (aw JEE uhn) stables were stables that the Greek hero Heracles had to clean as one of his twelve labors. He made the waters of two rivers flow through the stables and wash away the filth.

Avalon (AV uh lahn) in British legends was the island where King Arthur was carried after he died in battle. The legend says he will rise again to lead Britain.

B

Bard (bahrd) was a Celtic poet and singer in ancient times. A bard entertained people by making up and singing poems about brave deeds.

Battle of the Alamo (AL uh moh) was a battle between Texas settlers and Mexican forces when Texas was fighting for independence from Mexico. It took place at the Alamo, a fort in San Antonio, in 1836.

Bifrost (BEE fruhst) in Norse myths was a rainbow bridge that connected Asgard with the world of people.

Black Land in ancient Egypt was the area of fertile soil around the banks of the River Nile. Most people lived there.

Brer Rabbit (brair RAB iht) myths are African American stories about a rabbit who played tricks on his friends. The stories grew out of animal myths from Africa.

C

Canoe Mountain in a Maidu myth of North America was the mountain on which the evil Coyote took refuge from a flood sent to drown him.

Changeling (CHAYNG lihng) in Celtic myths was a fairy child who had been swapped with a human baby at birth. Changelings were usually lazy and clumsy.

Confucianism (kuhn FYOO shuhn IHZ uhm) is a Chinese way of life and religion. It is based on the teachings of Confucius, also known as Kong Fu Zi, and is more than 2,000 years old.

Creation myths (kree AY shuhn mihths) are myths that tell how the world began.

D

Dwarfs (dwawrfs) in Norse myths were small people of great power. They were skilled at making tools and weapons.

F

Fairies (FAIR eez) in Celtic myths were called the Little People. They are especially common in Irish legends, where they are called leprechauns.

Fomors (FOH wawrz) in Irish myths were hideous giants who invaded Ireland and were fought by Lug.

G

Giants (JY uhnts) in Norse myths were huge people who had great strength and great powers. They often struggled with the warrior gods of Asgard.

Gnome (nohm) was a small, odd-looking person in the myths of many civilizations. In Inca myths, for example, gnomes were tiny people with very big beards.

Golden Apples of the Hesperides (heh SPEHR uh deez) were apples of gold in a garden that only the Greek gods could enter. They were collected by the hero Heracles as one of his twelve labors.

Golden fleece was the fleece of a ram that the Greek hero Jason won after many adventures with his ship, Argo, and his companion sailors, the Argonauts.

Green Knoll (nohl) was the home of the Little People, or fairies, in Irish and Scottish myths.

J

Jotunheim (YUR toon hym) in Norse myths was the land of the giants.

L

Lion men in myths of Africa were humans who can turn themselves into lions.

Little People in Celtic legends and folk tales are fairies. They are often fine sword makers and blacksmiths.

M

Machu Picchu (MAH choo PEE choo) is the ruins of an ancient city built by the Inca in the Andes Mountains of Peru.

Medecolin (may day coh leen) were a tribe of evil sorcerers in the myths of Algonquian Native American people.

Medicine (MEHD uh sihn) **man** is a wise man or shaman who has special powers. Medicine men also appear as beings with special powers in myths of Africa and North and South America. Also see **Shaman.**

Midgard (MIHD gahrd) in Norse myths was the world of people.

Muspell (MOOS pehl) in Norse myths was part of the Underworld. It was a place of fire.

N

Nidavellir in Norse myths was the land of the dwarfs.

Niflheim in Norse myths was part of the Underworld. It included Hel, the kingdom of the dead.

Nirvana (nur VAH nuh) in the religion of Buddhism is a state of happiness that people find when they have freed themselves from wanting things. People who reach Nirvana no longer have to be reborn.

O

Oracle (AWRR uh kuhl) in ancient Greece was a sacred place served by people who could foretell the future. Greeks journeyed there to ask questions about their fortunes. Also see **Soothsayer.**

P

Pacariqtambo (pahk kah ree TAHM boh) in Inca myths was a place of three caves from which the first people stepped out into the world. It is also called Paccari Tampu.

Poppykettle was a clay kettle made for brewing poppyseed tea. In an Inca myth, a poppykettle was used for a boat.

Prophecy (PRAH feh see) is a prediction made by someone who foretells the future.

R

Ragnarok (RAHG nah ruhk) in Norse myths was the final battle of good and evil, in which the giants would fight against the gods of Asgard.

S

Sahara (sah HAH rah) is a vast desert that covers much of northern Africa.

Seriema was a bird in a Carajá myth of South America whose call led the first people to try to find their way from underground to the surface of the earth.

Shaman (SHAH muhn) can be a real person, a medicine man or wise person who knows the secrets of nature. Shamans also appear as beings with special powers in some myths of North and South America. Also see **Medicine man.**

Soothsayer (sooth SAY ur) in ancient Greece was someone who could see into the future. Also see **Oracle.**

Svartalfheim (SVAHRT uhl hym) in Norse myths was the home of the dark elves.

T

Tar Baby was a sticky doll made of tar used to trap Brer Rabbit, a tricky rabbit in African American folk tales.

Tara (TAH rah) in Irish myths was the high seat, or ruling place, of the Irish kings.

Trickster (TRIHK stur) **animals** are clever ones that appear in many myths of North America, South America, and Africa.

Trojan horse. See **Wooden horse of Troy.**

Tuatha dÈ Danann (THOO uh huh day DUH nuhn) were the people of the goddess Danu. Later they were known as gods of Ireland themselves.

V

Vanaheim (VAH nah hym) in Norse myths was the home of the fertility gods.

W

Wadjet eye was a symbol used by the people of ancient Egypt. It stood for the eye of the gods Ra and Horus and was supposed to bring luck.

Wheel of Transmigration (tranz my GRAY shuhn) in the religion of Buddhism is the wheel people's souls reach after they die. From there they are sent back to earth to be born into a higher or lower life.

Wooden horse of Troy was a giant wooden horse built by the Greeks during the Trojan War. The Greeks hid soldiers in the horse's belly and left the horse for the Trojans to find.

Y

Yang (yang) is the male quality of light, sun, heat, and dryness in Chinese beliefs. Yang struggles with Yin for control of things.

Yatkot was a magical tree in an African myth of the Alur people.

Yggdrasil (IHG drah sihl) in Norse myths was a mighty tree that held all three worlds together and reached up into the stars.

Yin (yihn) is the female quality of shadow, moon, cold, and water in Chinese beliefs. Yin struggles with Yang for control of things.

CUMULATIVE INDEX

This is an alphabetical list of important topics covered in all eight volumes of the **World Book Myths and Legends** series. Next to each entry is at least one pair of numbers separated by a slash mark (/). For example, the entry for Argentina is "**Argentina** 8/4". The first number tells you what volume to look in for information. The second number tells you what page you should turn to in that volume. Sometimes a topic appears in more than one place. When it does, additional volume and page numbers are given. Here's a reminder of the volume numbers and titles: 1, *African Myths and Legends;* 2, *Ancient Egyptian Myths and Legends;* 3, *Ancient Greek Myths and Legends;* 4, *Celtic Myths and Legends;* 5, *Chinese Myths and Legends;* 6, *Norse Myths and Legends;* 7, *North American Myths and Legends;* 8, *South American Myths and Legends.*

I

Icarus, son of Daedalus 3/20–21
Iguana Islands, home of the dragon lizards 8/40
Iliad, The 3/3
Inca, a South American people 8/3–5, 8/31–35, 8/37–41
Indians, American see **North American peoples**
Inuit, a North American people 7/5, 7/21–24
Iobates, king of Lycia 3/22–23
Iolas, cousin of Heracles 3/26
Irin-Mage, father of humankind 8/26–27
Iroquois, a North American people 7/11–15
Isis, goddess of fertility 2/5, 2/7–11, 2/21–23
   discovering Ra's secret name 2/43–47
   search for Osiris 2/13–17

J

Jade Emperor 5/45, 5/46
jaguar 8/13, 8/15–17
James I, King of England 8/5
Jason and the Argonauts 3/5, 3/37–41
jatoba, a tree 8/15, 8/46–47
Jocasta, queen of Thebes 3/43, 3/46–47
Jormungand, a serpent 6/3, 6/10–11, 6/19
Jotunheim, a Norse world 6/3

K

Ka, Island of 2/37–41
Kaboi, a very wise man 8/19, 8/23
Kayapó a South American people 8/3, 8/13–17
Kewawkqu', a race of giants and magicians 7/17
Khoi, an African people 1/13–17
Kigbo, a stubborn man 1/30–35
Knossos, palace of 3/14
Kodoyanpe, brother god of Coyote 7/43–46
Kuang Zi Lian, a rich merchant and farmer 5/31–35
Kui, an ugly scholar 5/37–41
Kvasir, a wise god 6/5, 6/44–47

L

Labors of Heracles 3/25–29
Labyrinth, of Daedalus 3/14–17, 3/20
Laeding, a special chain 6/20
Laius, king of Thebes 3/43–47
Lao Zi, founder of Taoism 5/5, 5/46
Li Xuan, one of the Eight Immortals 5/34–35
Light, child of Amma 1/18–20, 1/22, 1/23
lion men 1/42–47
Lizard, a prince 1/24–29
Loki, half giant, half god 6/4, 6/19
   Andvari's ring 6/13–16
   Balder's death 6/36–38
   his downfall 6/44–47
   in the land of the giants 6/7, 6/8, 6/10
   stolen hammer myth 6/29–33
Lord of Heaven 5/10

M

Ma'at, goddess of justice 2/45
macaw, a clever bird 8/7–10, 8/13–15
Machu Picchu, an ancient Inca city 8/38
Maidu myth 7/43–47

Maira-Monan, son of Irin-Mage 8/27–29
Mali myths 1/19–23, 1/43–47
Manco Capac, founder of the Inca 8/35
Manitou, an Iroquois god 7/12–14
Medea, daughter of King Aeëtes 3/39–41
Medecolin, a race of cunning sorcerers 7/17
medicine man 1/43–47
Medusa, the Gorgon 3/9, 3/22
Meginjardir, a magic belt 6/4, 6/7
Melcarthus, king of Byblos 2/14, 2/16
Mi Hun Tang, the Potion of Forgetting 5/26
Michabo, the Great Hare 7/6–9
Midas, king of Phrygia 3/7–8
Midgard, a Norse world 6/3, 6/9, 6/29
Minos, king of Crete 3/13–16, 3/20
Minotaur, half man, half bull 3/13–17, 3/20
missionaries 1/3
mistletoe trick 6/35–39
Mjollnir, Thor's magic hammer 6/4, 6/7, 6/29–33, 6/37, 6/42
Modgurd, a gatekeeper 6/42–43
Monan, Tupinamba creator god 8/25–27
Monkey, the most cunning of all monkeys 5/43–47
murder of Osiris 2/7–11
Muspell, a Norse world 6/3

N

Nanna, goddess wife of Balder 6/38, 6/42
Nanook, the white bear 7/23
Narcissus, a man who loved himself 3/10–11
Narve, son of Loki 6/46
Native American peoples see **North American peoples;**
   South American peoples
Neith, mother of Ra 2/23
Nekumonta, the Iroquois brave 7/10–15
Nemean lion 3/25
Nephthys, wife of Seth 2/17
Nidavellir, a Norse world 6/3
Nidhogg, a dragon 6/3
Niflheim, a Norse world 6/3, 6/19, 6/42–43
Niger, a river 1/46
Nigeria, home of the Yoruba 1/3, 1/4
Nile River 2/2
nirvana, a blissful state 5/5
Norse people 6/2–5
North American peoples 7/2–5
   native 7/2–5, 7/7–25, 7/43–47
   see also **African Americans; European settlers;**
   and individual tribes, e.g., **Inuit; Iroquois; Sioux**
Nu, a god 2/25–26
Nü Wa, Gourd Girl 5/7–11
Nut, the sky goddess 2/5
nymphs 3/9, 3/10–11, 3/33, 3/38

O

ochre, very red earth 2/27–29
Odin, chief of the gods 6/4, 6/25, 6/39, 6/41
   Andvari's ring 6/13–16
   downfall of Loki 6/44–47
   trapping the wolf, Fenris 6/19–22
Odysseus, a hero 3/3, 3/5, 3/31–32, 3/34
Odyssey, The 3/3

For information on other World Book products, visit our Web site at www.worldbook.com or call 1-800-WORLDBK (967-5325).

For information on sales to schools and libraries, call 1-800-975-3250.

Cover background illustration by Paul Perreault

Pages 48-64: ©2002 World Book, Inc. All rights reserved. WORLD BOOK and the GLOBE DEVICE are registered trademarks or trademarks of World Book, Inc. No part of this publication may be reproduced, stored in a retrieval system, or transmitted in any form or by any means electronic, mechanical, photocopying, recording, or otherwise, without prior written permission from the publisher.

World Book, Inc.
233 North Michigan Avenue
Chicago, IL 60601

Pages 1–47: format and illustrations, ©1997 Belitha Press; text, ©1997 Philip Ardagh

Printed in Hong Kong
2 3 4 5 6 7 8 9 10 10 09 08 07 06 05 04 03 02

ISBN(set): 0-7166-2613-6
African Myths and Legends
ISBN: 0-7166-2605-5
LC: 2001026492
Ancient Egyptian Myths and Legends
ISBN: 0-7166-2606-3
LC: 2001026501
Ancient Greek Myths and Legends
ISBN: 0-7166-2607-1
LC: 2001035959
Celtic Myths and Legends
ISBN: 0-7166-2608-X
LC: 20011026496
Chinese Myths and Legends
ISBN: 0-7166-2609-8
LC: 2001026489
Norse Myths and Legends
ISBN: 0-7166-2610-1
LC: 2001026488
North American Myths and Legends
ISBN: 0-7166-2611-X
LC: 2001026490
South American Myths and Legends
ISBN: 0-7166-2612-8
LC: 2001026491